SpringerBriefs in E

We are delighted to announce SpringerBriefs in Education, an innovative product type that combines elements of both journals and books. Briefs present concise summaries of cutting-edge research and practical applications in education. Featuring compact volumes of 50 to 125 pages, the SpringerBriefs in Education allow authors to present their ideas and readers to absorb them with a minimal time investment. Briefs are published as part of Springer's eBook Collection. In addition, Briefs are available for individual print and electronic purchase.

SpringerBriefs in Education cover a broad range of educational fields such as: Science Education, Higher Education, Educational Psychology, Assessment & Evaluation, Language Education, Mathematics Education, Educational Technology, Medical Education and Educational Policy.

SpringerBriefs typically offer an outlet for:

- An introduction to a (sub)field in education summarizing and giving an overview of theories, issues, core concepts and/or key literature in a particular field
- A timely report of state-of-the art analytical techniques and instruments in the field of educational research
- A presentation of core educational concepts
- An overview of a testing and evaluation method
- A snapshot of a hot or emerging topic or policy change
- An in-depth case study
- A literature review
- A report/review study of a survey
- An elaborated thesis

Both solicited and unsolicited manuscripts are considered for publication in the SpringerBriefs in Education series. Potential authors are warmly invited to complete and submit the Briefs Author Proposal form. All projects will be submitted to editorial review by editorial advisors.

SpringerBriefs are characterized by expedited production schedules with the aim for publication 8 to 12 weeks after acceptance and fast, global electronic dissemination through our online platform SpringerLink. The standard concise author contracts guarantee that:

- an individual ISBN is assigned to each manuscript
- each manuscript is copyrighted in the name of the author
- the author retains the right to post the pre-publication version on his/her website or that of his/her institution

More information about this series at http://www.springer.com/series/8914

Merlin B. Thompson

Fundamentals of Piano Pedagogy

Fuelling Authentic Student Musicians
from the Beginning

 Springer

Merlin B. Thompson
Schulich School of Music
McGill University
Montréal, QC
Canada

and

Werklund School of Education
University of Calgary
Calgary, AB
Canada

ISSN 2211-1921   ISSN 2211-193X   (electronic)
SpringerBriefs in Education
ISBN 978-3-319-65532-1   ISBN 978-3-319-65533-8   (eBook)
DOI 10.1007/978-3-319-65533-8

Library of Congress Control Number: 2017949495

This Springer imprint is published by Springer Nature
The registered company is Springer International Publishing AG
The registered company address is: Gewerbestrasse 11, 6330 Cham, Switzerland

*This book is dedicated
to my students and their parents,
to my family, friends, and colleagues.
Your interest and understanding
made it all possible.*

Contents

Chapter 1
Introduction

Abstract This brief introductory chapter sets the tone for a humanistic and holistic educational exploration by asserting that meaningful studio music instruction encompasses multiple layers of teacher involvement. This means music teaching is more than mere transmission of musical knowledge and skills. Meaningful music instruction builds on the powerful yet natural connection we have individually and universally with music. It's driven by students' own interests, by their need to thrive as autonomous learners who value exploration, creation, and mastery. Further, it relies on teachers who engage students as active participants by tapping into relevant teaching and learning research, their awareness of others and life experiences, and their own musical expertise. They serve as spark to their students' musical flame right from the very beginning.

Week after week and year after year, piano teachers help their students make rewarding and challenging connections with music. Like their vocal and instrumental studio music colleagues, the piano teacher's influence is no more important than at the beginning—those first four to five years during which students initiate, investigate, and expand their own musical mastery. So, how might piano teachers fuel successful student participation and growth? What do teachers need to know about piano pedagogy right from the very beginning?

This book is all about the *fundamentals* of piano pedagogy—the foundational ideas that empower teachers in their working with beginner students. Fundamentals have an anchoring quality that I appreciate because they provide much-needed stability and confidence for teaching and learning. Fundamentals encompass multiple layers of support, background, basics, and origin. Yet, they also foster a feeling of genesis and the energetic dynamism that assists growth and development. In the pages following, I examine and articulate the personal, philosophical, educational, practical, and performance underpinnings teachers need to nurture meaningful development in their students. To accomplish this task, I draw on music philosophers, giants of the performance world, current research in music education, and my own experience of working with enquiring colleagues and hundreds of students from around the world.

© The Author(s) 2018
M.B. Thompson, *Fundamentals of Piano Pedagogy*,
SpringerBriefs in Education, DOI 10.1007/978-3-319-65533-8_1

Fundamentals of Piano Pedagogy differs from other music education sources by building on three distinctive instructional dynamics. Namely, that meaningful music instruction is always:

- *Based on our relation with music.* Musical relationships encompass everything from intense involvement to casual exploration to complete distraction. This means music teaching is more than mere transmission of musical knowledge and skills. It's about helping students uncover more of their individual relations with music.
- *Driven by students' interests.* Students thrive as autonomous learners who value exploration, creation, and mastery. This means teaching goes beyond passive student repetition of performance drills. It's about actively engaging students in their own meaningful learning.
- *Guided by teachers' expertise.* Teachers are more than assertive authorities who control students' awareness of what's wrong or right. Because teachers have vast musical and instructional knowledge, they're able to lead students when they cannot lead themselves, pass on the musical tools students need, and expand students' ongoing relation with music.

Fundamentals of Piano Pedagogy provides a thoughtful response to the gap created by a history of prioritizing music performance over music teaching and the contemporary trend for prescriptive repertoire-based and activity-based teaching. As an alternative, this book stands out as a much-needed instructional resource with immense personal, practical, social, philosophical, educational, and cultural relevance for today's studio music teachers. It offers teachers a deep understanding of teaching from the beginning and invites them to consider their multilayered role in uplifting musical adventures—ones that require thinking not only about who they are and what music means to them, but also what they have yet to imagine about themselves, about music, their students, and life.

I begin this exploration in Chap. 2 by examining three themes that may initiate and sustain the first four to five years of teaching beginner piano students: our relation with music, student independence, and personal authenticity. Firstly, our relation with music spans an entire spectrum of experiences from music performance, to critical thinking, to playing around. Knowing that it's difficult to sustain music study by doing the same thing at the same level for long periods of time, teachers incorporate diverse aspects from our relation with music to ensure meaningful ongoing musical development. Secondly, student independence emerges from children's natural inclination to do things on their own. Given that students may take ownership of desirable skills and knowledge as well as undesirable drawbacks, teachers use a process of multiple ownership to help students develop awareness of their own performance. Finally, personal authenticity refers to the notion of being true to oneself. By understanding, accepting, and caring for students' true self at all levels and ages, teachers may reinforce the genuine connection between who students are and what they do as musicians.

In order to help teachers understand what happens when beginner piano students take their initial steps, Chap. 3 examines the concept of learning from several relevant perspectives. Firstly, an overview of education theories indicates that learning is frequently interpreted as involving: (1) linear progressions, (2) making meaning from experience, (3) cyclical processes focused on exploration, and (4) the influence of individual and collective worldviews. Next, given the parallels between language learning and music learning, this chapter explores the process of language acquisition and transposes the principles of language learning to music learning. Finally, this chapter demonstrates how beginner piano students may move through three fundamental stages of musical development. The Background Stage involves how students informally acquire aspects of musicianship prior to formal lessons. The Foundation Stage focuses on tonalization development of technique and tone production as well as learning to play by ear. The Reading Stage continues to build on the Foundation Stage through the additional element of learning to read music.

Teaching beginner piano students is an endeavor that builds implicitly and explicitly on teachers' beliefs, musical ideals, and personal values. Chapter 4 begins by exploring how many twenty-first century teaching resources and practices have their origins in the piano's history, influential educational movements, as well as scientific and industrial developments of the 1800s. As alternatives to this pedagogic history, teachers may incorporate principles of democracy and parenting as models for instruction—two approaches that highlight how teaching is concerned with the relationships between teachers and students. Democratic music teachers draw from the ideals of freedom, equality, and dignity to solicit their students' thoughts and opinions. They're purposeful in finding out what students think, rather than looking for students to regurgitate what teachers think. Democratic teaching emphasizes how the teacher's role has inherently moral and ethical undertones. The parenting model highlights how teachers take on overlapping yet distinct roles. They provide leadership when students don't know the way. They hand over the musical tools students need for successful musical learning. And, they provide the impetus for expanding students' ongoing mastery of musicianship.

Chapter 5 focuses on piano tone and technique—two inseparable aspects of teachers' work with beginner piano students. Historically, tone has been considered as a most essential ingredient in the world of music because mastery of tone production enables artistic expression. This chapter examines how tone may be characterized as sound vibrations—intensities of energy—that range from soft to loud, light to heavy, bright to dark, short to long, flat to round, and more. Pianists bring immense variations in tonal intensity to their performances by tapping into their emotional, spiritual, intellectual, intuitive, and physical energies. In a departure from treating piano technique as a kind of mechanical training, this chapter considers piano technique as something we may already know about because of how we use our fingers, hands, arms, and body in ordinary everyday life. Specific examples of how beginner piano students may explore five technical basics include: grabbing fingers, walking fingers, arm circles, our body, and appropriate posture at the piano.

In Chap. 6, I address the notion of teaching the student as different from teaching the repertoire. This approach specifically involves the teacher's ability to go beyond the repertoire to stimulate comprehensive student musical development. Also relevant to the aspect of teaching students is the accumulated repertoire approach wherein students review and refine pieces they know how to play, instead of dropping pieces after they've been learned. Teaching the student may also require teachers to consider their roles as student advocators and agitators. Advocating is all about welcoming students into unconditional learning processes that respect students' personality. As agitators, teachers challenge their students by taking them beyond their comfort zone. Finally, this chapter examines what happens when students' concern shifts from fulfilling their own self-interests to care for the wellbeing of music.

Researchers have repeatedly affirmed that parental interest in their children's musical development has a noticeably positive impact on children's musical development even without parents having any musical knowledge. Knowing that parents and teachers naturally bring different yet overlapping perspectives to beginner piano students, Chap. 7 considers the relation between teachers and parents. An examination of interactions between teachers and parents from a historical perspective and within musical settings reveals that teachers may unconsciously perpetuate attitudes of assumed teacher authority over parents. As an alternative, teachers may establish meaningful parent relations by developing openness and trust that includes listening to what parents have to contribute, figuring out what they need, finding out what works, and drawing from what's already there rather than trying to reconfigure the family's structure. This chapter concludes by providing practical information for the first conversation with parents, musical cornerstones for parents, welcoming real life families, and twice-yearly teacher-parent interviews.

I've written *Fundamentals of Piano Pedagogy* with several audiences in mind. Firstly, as the textbook for undergraduate piano performance majors interested in studio music instruction. My goal is to provide pianists with an instructional approach reflective of twenty-first century education research, contemporary cultural values, and proven music instructional strategies. Secondly, as a resource for novice and veteran piano teachers. My goal is to provide teachers with an examination of the issues regarding piano teaching that surfaced in my own teaching and the essential questions from years of discussions and workshops with teachers. Thirdly, as a resource for vocal and non-keyboard instrumental music teachers. My goal is to provide studio music teachers with a framework of effective teaching principles that empowers teachers in working with beginner music students.

Studio music teachers play an essential role in students' musical development because they bring multiple traits and expertise to learning and teaching. Through their passion for music, pedagogical insight, educational understanding, awareness of others, and life knowledge, teachers serve as a spark to their students' musical flame. They purposefully ignite and fuel another person's thriving relation with music. I hope that *Fundamentals of Piano Pedagogy* will assist teachers in working through, developing, stretching, inquiring, and honoring the multilayered practice of teaching right from the very beginning.

Chapter 2
Themes to Initiate and Sustain the Journey

Abstract Teachers may initiate and sustain the first four to five years of teaching beginner piano students by drawing upon three foundational themes: our relation with music, student independence, and personal authenticity. Firstly, our relation with music spans an entire spectrum of experiences from music performance, to critical thinking, to playing around. Knowing that it's difficult to sustain music study by doing the same thing at the same level for long periods of time, teachers incorporate diverse aspects from our relation with music to ensure meaningful ongoing musical development. Secondly, student independence emerges from children's natural inclination to do things on their own. Given that students may take ownership of desirable skills and knowledge as well as undesirable drawbacks, teachers use a process of multiple ownership to help students develop awareness of their own performance. Finally, personal authenticity refers to the notion of students' being true to oneself. By understanding, accepting, and caring for students' true self at all levels and ages, teachers may reinforce the genuine connection between who students are and what they do as musicians.

Not long ago, I attended one of my former student's B.Mus. graduation concert. It was wonderful to hear and see how much she was still the same delightful performer I'd always known and how she'd grown in her sophistication as a musician. After the concert, I couldn't help thinking about how people and events shape our lives, about how my parents, teachers, and colleagues helped set the stage for my own personal and professional explorations. Yet, when I graduated from university and decided to become a piano teacher, there were certain questions I needed to answer for myself. Questions like: How would my teaching reflect who I am? How would I view my students? What would I draw from to initiate and sustain the long journey of working with my students?

When I think about what anchors the first four to five years of working with beginner piano students, three enduring themes come into focus: our relation with music, student independence, and personal authenticity. These themes provide what pianist and pedagogue Swinkin (2015) referred to as a "pedagogical background" consisting of my core musical and non-musical beliefs and values that underlie and

M.B. Thompson, *Fundamentals of Piano Pedagogy*,
SpringerBriefs in Education, DOI 10.1007/978-3-319-65533-8_2

unify everything I do as a teacher (p. 9). While these themes were present right from my very first attempts at teaching, my awareness of them has most certainly evolved over 40 years of teaching. First and foremost, I place our relation with music at the top of my list because I believe that teaching and learning to play the piano may be best understood through the experience of music in our lives. Knowing about the various nuances and implications associated with our musical relations seems essential to developing students' musicianship. Next, I value student independence. I appreciate how students take ownership of music and learning. My responsibility is to incorporate their independence, add to it, and fill in the gaps as appropriate. Finally, personal authenticity—the notion of being true to oneself—is essential to my teaching. I pay close attention to my students' authentic self by recognizing and accepting who they genuinely are.

2.1 Our Relation with Music

Whether we're performing or playing, listening or creating, music punctuates our lives in a myriad of ways. From the random spontaneity of tapping a rhythm or humming a tune, to the formalized occasions of singing the national anthem or playing in a concert, these are all examples of how music fills our lives. Music has unlimited potential to make life more rich, enjoyable, and meaningful. As pianist Sylvia Coats offered, "Music touches the emotions. It makes us more fully human. One's primary reason for studying music is to enrich one's soul. Music provides solace in times of grief and enrichment in our everyday lives" (2006, p. 19). So, what exactly is going on when we consider our relation with music? How do people experience music in their lives?

One thing that makes our relation with music so remarkable may be expressed as the notion of flow—the optimal yet simple state of mind when things seem to come together. As described by renowned psychologist Csikszentmihalyi in his book *Flow* (1991), an activity that produces flow may be so gratifying that people willingly pursue it for its own sake, with little concern for what they will get out of it. In experiences involving flow, consciousness is harmoniously ordered, life is meaningful and enjoyable despite adversity (pp. 6–7). Based on worldwide research into what makes an experience genuinely satisfying, Csikszentmihalyi observed that people consistently identify flow with a complete range of experiences. At one end, flow occurs because the task undertaken has clear goals and provides immediate feedback—like playing the piano. While at the other end, flow is the result of an effortless involvement that removes the person from the worries and frustrations of everyday life—like playing the piano. Persons experiencing flow have a sense of control over their actions, while paradoxically concern for his or her self often disappears. Yet, the person's sense of self emerges stronger after the flow experience is over. With flow, there's often a sense that time has been altered, wherein hours pass by in minutes, and minutes can stretch out to seem like hours—like playing the piano. Finally, Csikszentmihalyi noticed that no person can sustain flow by doing the same thing at the same level for long periods of time (p. 75)—just like playing the piano.

Similar to the way flow involves a complete range of experiences, our relation with music also spans an entire spectrum. This means that on certain occasions, as music educator Jorgensen indicated, critical thinking takes priority in musical experiences. Here, our senses, intellect, and emotions are implicated in moments of deep concentration on the musical task at hand (2008, p. 23). On other occasions as extolled by Pollei, founding member of the American Piano Quartet, the benefits of noodling and fiddling come into play as the preferred route to musicianship (1991, p. 54). This is where freedom from worry in terms of playing around and taking boundless risks takes the lead. While from another viewpoint, the piano icon Schnabel proposed, "If I were a dictator, I would eliminate the term 'practice' from the vocabulary, for it becomes a bogy, a nightmare to children. I would ask them: 'Have you already made and enjoyed music today? If not—go and make music'" (Schnabel 1945/1962, p. 162). Schnabel encourages each of us to dive into the joy of making music.

Because students naturally seek out and participate in diverse meaningful musical experiences, it makes sense for teachers to incorporate diversities like playing around, making music, and thinking critically about performance development—three examples from the spectrum of our relation with music that have profound influences on each other. By playing around and risk taking, students may find out what they don't know or cannot do; so, that necessitates bringing in critical thinking, which may lead to explicit actions; which might need to be tested out in musical performance or more playing around. In this context, teachers recognize why students may get tired of critical thinking. They know why students may become disinterested in intentional music making and even the aspects of playing or fiddling around. As a consequence, teachers and students avoid falling victim to the dangers of repeatedly doing the same thing at the same level for extended periods of time.

Teachers play a pivotal role in supporting and extending students' own spectrum of musical relations. This means piano teachers do more than merely transmitting musical knowledge and skills; they use students' individual relation with music to stimulate and support their ongoing musical development. They take advantage of the broad spectrum that is our relation with music because as music educator Allsup has proposed, "we are more than makers of music; we are made by the music we make" (2016, p. 11).

2.2 Student Independence

Early in my teaching career, the following question from a parent had a major impact on my instructional approach.

"Just how long will it be before my child is able to practice on his own?"
I remember wondering—Was this question concerned with parental
involvement? What did the parent really want to know? Then it occurred to
me, this parent's question was all about my own role as teacher. More particularly, he wanted to know how my teaching approach would address his
own child's independence and ownership.
I replied, "Well, I think you'll be pleasantly surprised to see how many things
your child can do on his own even after the very first lesson!" And with that
simple statement, an adventurous exploration involving student independence
and ownership was underway.

Philosophers, educators, and child experts have long identified independence as a
natural dynamic in the child's growth from infancy to adulthood. From Rousseau
(1712–78), to Pestalozzi (1746–1827), to Montessori (1870–1952) and such current
parenting professionals as Barbara Coloroso, child independence is acknowledged
as an unavoidable and necessary element of every child's natural growth. We all
recognize the two-year-old's penchant for the word "No", the child's ongoing and
irrepressible drive to do things "My way", the rebellious teenager's need to separate
his or her self from family and eventually from peers as the inevitable signs of child
independence. In our Western cultural context, independence takes on a particular
relevance because, as social analyst Nisbett (2004) explained, there is an expec-
tation that each person is a "unitary free agent" personally charged with making the
most out of his or her life.

From the very earliest ages, children make amazing demonstrations of their
independence as musicians. Just think about how many children sing songs on their
own, move their bodies to the beat, and differentiate one musical selection from
another or one instrument from another. While children may acquire such fundamentals through direct instruction from adults, children's ownership of their
musicianship results mostly from their ordinary everyday encounters with music.
Music is something they internalize because of their preference for listening
repeatedly to certain musical selections. Their independent ownership of music
grows because children's daily lives are full of repetitious musical moments like
commercial jingles, church music, Christmas carols, Happy Birthday, music on the
radio, video games, movies, and more. In this way, children's musicianship isn't
something that develops randomly or just by chance. Nor is it something that only
develops in formal educational settings. Children take ownership of their own
musicianship as the result of listening to music and trying things out for themselves.

Teachers may build on their students' independence by recognizing, validating,
and following up on what students actually do—whether it's a matter of listening,
practicing, or reading, whether it's concerned with tone, technical fluency, or
interpretation. That means that while teachers take a leadership role in the early
stages as students become familiar with musical vocabulary and our way of

communicating, such processes are only fully successful when students take ownership of what's going on. Teachers play an important role in promoting students' "active participation in learning" (Niemi et al. 2012, p. 277) and allowing students to take responsibility for their own "personal decision-making" (Kemp and Mills 2002, p. 13). Even at the first lesson, teachers may prioritize students' ownership of sitting too high and just right, light and harsh tone, stiff and flexible fingers. As students progress as independent musicians, teachers make sure students take ownership of increasingly sophisticated musical concepts.

One of the challenges teachers face in supporting student independence is that students frequently take ownership of drawbacks like wrong notes, inflexible techniques, spontaneous fingerings, or radical interpretations. This challenge brings attention to a very pertinent issue: How can teachers minimize performance drawbacks while supporting student ownership? Teachers may address this issue by incorporating what I call *multiple ownership*. The goal in using multiple ownership is to heighten students' awareness of what they're doing, so they know how it differs from what might be preferable as demonstrated in the following examples.

> When Jessica started reading her pieces, she frequently played left hand chords in the wrong octave or E-G-C instead of C-E-G. Practicing with a multiple ownership approach meant exploring both correct and incorrect versions, comparing the sounds, and affirming placement on the keyboard.
>
> During her second piano lesson, Victoria achieved a legato sound by dropping her wrist and pushing her fingers into the keys. Rather than asking Victoria to discard her legato accomplishment, a multiple ownership approach allowed Victoria to compare how various wrist positions—low, high, stiff, light—impact her tone quality and physical fluency at the piano.
>
> Jeffrey often ran out of fingers in pieces that contained scale passages, spontaneously adding 4-5-4-5 in ascending, and 2-1-2-1 in descending right hand passages. Using a multiple ownership approach, he was able to explore formal alternatives and his own spontaneous versions, comparing their facility, and highlighting the necessary transitional fingers.
>
> Scott preferred to end all his pieces with a brusque *sforzando* on the last note. Using a multiple ownership approach meant trying out various ways to have fun with the ends of his pieces: getting softer, slowing down, speeding up, and of course suddenly loud.

Multiple ownership allows students to develop broader understanding of how their practice impacts their accomplishments. Rather than thinking of performance drawbacks as something to avoid, I consider drawbacks as an opportunity to expand students' awareness beyond their current ownership. As pianist and educator William Westney described in *The Perfect Wrong Note* (2003), "Sometimes we have to experience fully what's wrong in order to understand and integrate what's right, and honest mistakes are the only way to do that. They give texture to the act of learning" (pp. 63–64). Also in support of multiple ownership, author of *How We Learn* (2015) Benedict Carey proposed that varied practice has immense benefits over repetition of singular drills. Carey explains that *interleaving*—a cognitive science word that refers to the mixing of items, skills or concepts during practice—"seems to help us not only see the distinctions between them but also to achieve a clearer grasp of each one individually" (p. 164). Mixed-up practice builds overall dexterity and prompts active discrimination. The hardest part may be abandoning our primal faith in isolated repetition because, of course, everyone needs a certain amount of repetition to become familiar with any new skill or material. However, Carey suggests that repetition creates a powerful illusion because skills improve and then plateau. By contrast, varied practice produces a slower rate of improvement in each practice session but a greater accumulation of skill and learning over time.

While multiple ownership has its obvious merits, some teachers may fear that validating drawbacks will derail the learning process. Yet, in my own experience, I've observed that students' musicianship may survive and even flourish despite the arrival of wrong notes, inflexible techniques, and radical interpretations. Knowing that students frequently take ownership of things that may impede their learning, some teachers solve this problem by administering absolute control over students' musical development. Other teachers seem to regard independence as something only they can grant or bestow, and put off student ownership as a distant destination. These kinds of teaching seem to be embedded in a fear that students' independence or ownership will result in teachers' loss of control. Or, teachers may feel compelled to streamline student development in ways that avoid moving outside teachers' comfort zone. However, under such circumstances, it's questionable how the weight of teacher authority will avoid fostering students' blind complacency or outright dislike.

Finally, students' processes of taking ownership have both independent and dependent implications. From the independent perspective, taking ownership is something that emerges from the child's own natural inclination to do things on his or her own without assistance. It comes from the child's inherent yearning to separate his or her self from family, peers, and teachers. In this respect, students' independence is anchored in their sense of self. While from the dependent perspective, students also depend on teachers to recognize what they achieve on their own and to introduce what they cannot find on their own. They rely on teachers to guide their musical development without squashing their highly valued sense of independence. Under such circumstances, students' growing musicianship might be described as a process of *dependent independence*. That's why it's important for teachers not only to recognize students' knowledge and sense of ownership, it's also important to challenge and expand student independence, to keep in mind where we're going and how teachers may assist students in getting there.

2.3   Personal Authenticity

> Around the time energetic Arthur was in preschool, his older sister Janine informed me he would soon be starting lessons. "My Mom really hopes that piano lessons will help to settle him down", she told me. I couldn't stop myself from thinking that both Janine and her Mom might be disappointed by the outcome of Arthur's lessons. Because, my goal wouldn't be to reduce, minimize, or eliminate Arthur's boisterous authentic self. It would be a matter of amplifying who Arthur is as a person—his personal authenticity.

As criteria for musical performance, the term authenticity is often used regarding the composer's performance intentions, faithfulness to historical performance, and period sound especially in terms of techniques and instruments.[1] So, let me begin by stating that's not what I intend to explore in this segment. My purpose is to examine authenticity from a personal perspective especially as concerned with the notion of being true to oneself. Personal authenticity is all about the way in which a person's actions genuinely align with his or her authentic self—that is the many layers that make up each person's uniqueness much like a fabric woven from the countless threads of who we are. Being personally authentic relies on connecting the fabric of *who* we are and *what* we value about ourselves with *how* we actually get on with life. For teachers, paying attention to students' authentic self involves understanding, recognizing, accepting, and caring for who they are, rather than controlling who we might want them to be.

Throughout history, poets and philosophers have repeatedly acknowledged the importance of personal authenticity. From the 400 BC inscription *"Know yourself"* on the Temple of Apollo in Delphi, to the 4th century St. Augustine's *"In the inward man dwells truth"*, to Shakespeare's 16th century *"To thine own self be true"*, and contemporary educator Carl Roger's expression *"Be yourself"*, these phrases represent the long historical trajectory of concern for knowing, listening, and being true to our own internal voice. As Canadian philosopher Taylor (1991) described,

> There is a certain way of being human that is my way. I am called up to live my life in this way, and not in imitation of anyone else's. But this gives a new importance to being true to myself. If I am not, I miss the point of my life, I miss what being human is for *me* (p. 29).

Personal authenticity brings clarity and meaning to who we are and what we do in life. Without authenticity, there may be a sense of superficiality, artificiality, or disconnection from life. With authenticity, we may experience both comfort and discomfort in being true to oneself—when on certain occasions it's easy to tap into our own personal authenticity, and elsewhere when we're challenged to remain true

---

[1]See Swinkin (2015, pp. 54–55) and Kivy (2002, pp. 238–250) for summaries regarding interpretation and critique of the authentic music performance movement.

to who we are. Yet, we take on both comfort and discomfort associated with being true to oneself, as philosophers and poets throughout history have indicated, because of the value and meaning we take from our own authentic self.[2]

Music serves as a resonant and intimate vehicle for experiencing who we are and how we actually get on with life. As music philosopher Cumming (2000) explained, the musician's individuality is "inseparable from the sounds she makes" (p. 27). Musicians express who they are because music's technical, expressive, explorative, and formal demands prompt all varieties and intensities of personal involvement. Similarly, in educational processes, the ideal of authenticity receives widespread support because educational activities take on personal meaning when connected to the person's true or core self.[3] So, this brings us to consider: How might an understanding of authenticity impact musical study and performance? What happens when teachers pay attention to the student's authentic self?

Music lessons provide teachers with ample ongoing opportunities to interact one-on-one with their students for periods that may span several years of weekly involvement from preschool through high school. Teachers get to know their student's authentic self through observing and listening on professional, casual, immediate, and introspective levels. Everything comes into play. Things like the physicality of what students do—the quickness or slowness of how students move, mannerisms, the flexibility in bodily involvement and digital finesse, physical strength, the comfort of a balanced body, what their eyes do, body language, breathing and gestures, the need for movement. Students have their own emotional compass—easily frustrated, endless patience, playing from the heart, how things feel, dealing with success and failure, openness to all kinds of emotional intent. There's everything connected with thinking—brief and lengthy concentration, making sense of what's going on, the words they use, their own life experiences, short and long term goals, how much they have to say, figuring out the meaning of progress and setbacks. Students possess their own intuitive insight—being in the moment, spontaneous creativity and imagination, letting go and trusting your gut. Things like spirituality—soulful grounding, anima mundi, faith, what students believe in, morals, what they care about, relation to nature, cultural and community values. In the context of studio music lessons, teachers put together a picture of their students' true self as a result of immediate and evolving perceptions. They assemble information from students' interactions with their teachers, other students, and their parents. They witness how the fabric of students' core self is indelibly

---

[2]Personal authenticity is not without its critics. Aloni (2002) warned that authenticity tied solely to the subjective self may create a "nihilistic position according to which everything is equally good and beautiful and just as long as the individual's choice was authentic" (p. 104). Theoretical researchers (Barry et al. 2011; Hotchkiss 2002) and social commentators (Lasch 1979; Wolfe 1976) have argued against the narcissistic qualities of individualism associated with a liberal, affluent, secular, and consumer-oriented North American culture.

[3]On the topic of authenticity in educational settings see: Brookfield (2006), Cranton (2001), Kreber (2013), Palmer (1998), Rogers (1969).

woven into their relation with music, the sounds they make, the interpretations they prefer, the way they learn, the tools they use to study and perform, the spontaneous expression of their own internal voice. Here are a few snapshots of my beginner and elementary students taken through an authentic lens:

> Jennifer is soft-spoken with a keen desire to express her sense of humor. Her subtle jokes often provide openings for exploration of both familiar and unfamiliar musical avenues.
>
> Alex only talks about music in terms of how it makes him feel. His ability as a composer, perfect pitch, and playing by ear stand in direct contrast to his discomfort with learning to read music.
>
> Everything about Erica sparkles: her eyes, her speech patterns, her clothes, her gestures. She has a penchant for jumping into her performances, often charging headstrong through entire sections without a single breath.
>
> The combination of Brandon's confidence in his own intuition and urge for self-mastery often results in elevated frustration. He rarely gives up.

Recognizing each of my student's authentic self has important implications related to his or her musical growth especially in terms of two vital areas: triggering interest and developing expertise. Interest may be described as the feeling of curiosity or desire for exploration that compels a person to experiment or willingly take risks. Often the delight associated with interest involves breaking through boundaries, challenging established rules, or stepping beyond a person's comfort zone. Expertise may be defined as know-how that exceeds the demands of a given task. It's the competency, skills, and knowledge that equip a person to successfully complete activities within a certain area. Confidence associated with expertise typically results from a person working within the broad base of his or her own comfort zone.

While interest and expertise both help to define who we genuinely are, they draw from the fabric of our own true self in significantly different ways. Quite remarkably, the curiosity associated with interest involves stepping outside our own comfort zone, while expertise builds from within our own comfort zone. Although interest and expertise may occupy opposite ends of the spectrum, personal interest often generates the commitments of time and energy necessary to produce expertise. Expertise relies on a person's interest in doing something well, and personal interest stimulates adjustments to a person's expertise.

In order to tap into students' interest and expertise, teachers may need not only to understand and recognize their students, but also accept and care for who their students are. Accepting a student's true self is an unconditional and nonjudgmental practice that speaks of openness and humility. Acceptance isn't about changing a student's authentic self into something else. It's about caring for the genuine fabric of a student's true self. Teachers who genuinely accept their students' personal authenticity open themselves to personally care about their students by involving students in their own learning journey, by protecting them, and by shielding students from excessive demands. They know when and how to guard students' vulnerability. Yet, accepting and caring for students also means teachers know when to take risks and when not, when it's appropriate to push students out of their comfort zone and urge students to look beyond their immediate vision. In this latter example, teachers help keep students from being held hostage by their own defensive sense of self. They recognize that knowing students' authentic self isn't about ego building or doing only what students want. It's about teachers becoming skilled advocates on their students' behalf, supporting and challenging students' true self.

Teaching with personal authenticity means teachers value who their students are. They guide their students by exploring musicianship as something unequivocally and enduringly grounded in students' own true self. This is not to underrate the influence of teachers' own authentic self, their own interests, expertise, wisdom, or practical experience. Obviously, teachers' input is vitally important. However, in acknowledging students' true self, teachers may provide leadership without taking over their students' journeys. In this process, teachers promote a flourishing of their students' inner voices—not as something previously unknown, mere teacher imitation, or something students eventually achieve. Rather, teachers inspire and validate the inner voices that were already there and that continue to drive students' own evolving and highly personal relation to music.

2.4 Final Thoughts

This chapter began with several thought provoking questions. How would my teaching reflect who I am? How would I view my students? What would I draw from to initiate and sustain the long journey of working with my students? From these questions, themes of our relation with music, student independence, and personal authenticity have emerged to initiate and sustain my teaching for over thirty years. What's interesting about this trio of themes is how they represent a particular aspect of teaching that might be referred to as—*what is*. While, at the same time, they also signify a contrasting aspect of teaching that might be described as—*what might be*.[4]

---

[4]In a similar vein Swinkin (2015) proposed that teachers may take on a transformative stance wherein their prime imperative is to open up new and numerous possibilities for the student (pp. 222–23). Allsup (2016) addressed possibilities from another angle, suggesting teachers are directed to "something just outside the possible" (p. 141).

I use the expression *what is* to describe our massive accumulation of knowledge and experience. It's things we already know, what we do right now, where we are, and where we've come from. From a musical perspective, *what is* encompasses the musical traditions that surround us, the instruments we play, what students bring to their musicianship, teachers' backgrounds and expertise, educational attitudes and trends, our societal and individual values. *What is* embodies where we are right now —musically, personally, and in life. In contrast, the expression *what might be* taps into the vastness of things we have yet to imagine. *What might be* directs us toward expanding the space of what's possible, uncovering what no one has ever thought of before. What I find remarkable is that teaching *what is* and *what might be* are not unrelated instructional strategies. Teaching isn't just about getting acquainted with or mastering *what is*. Nor is teaching just about uncovering *what might be*. Teaching may be understood as the deliberate and repeatedly cyclical process of opening up spaces of personal possibility by exploring where we are right now. Teaching *what is* serves as the excellent foundation and active inspiration for uncovering *what might be*. For what piano teacher and author Barbara Skalinder described as "drawing out the possibility in every student" (2016, p. 137).

What stands out for me in this exploration is how our relation with music, student independence, and personal authenticity may stimulate infinite possibilities. As a teacher, I am greatly influenced by the musical traditions I carry forward. That means I pass on the breadth of musicianship with immense dedication and purpose. Yet, my teaching isn't so much about perpetuating entrenched ways of thinking about music as it is about teaching *what is* and *what might be* in order to broaden what students come to know, feel, and do as musicians. On this view, music teachers emphasize two things. Firstly and perhaps most obviously, that music teaching is devoted to fostering and upholding the value we have for music and artistic meaning making. While secondly and perhaps with less apparent intentions, music teaching embodies a grand adventure that pulls each of us to consider not only who we are and where we come from, but also what we have yet to imagine about ourselves, about each other, about music, and about life.

2.5 Before We Move on

1. What comes to mind when you examine your own relation with music? How does the idea of flow as a range of personal experiences come into play in your musical experiences? How might the combination of critical thinking and playing around contribute to your teaching and learning to play a musical instrument?
2. What is your own experience of independence? How might you apply what you've learned about independence and ownership in this chapter to your own teaching? What changes will you make?

3. By understanding, accepting, and caring for their students' authentic self at all levels and ages, teachers reinforce the meaningful connection between who students are and what they do as musicians. How do you feel about this statement? What stands out for you?

4. This chapter concluded by suggesting that teaching *what is* serves as the excellent foundation and active inspiration for uncovering *what might be*. Which is more comfortable for you as a teacher—*What is*? Or *what might be*? Why?

5. Your own musical autobiography consists of the many musical events, moments, and experiences that occurred over your lifetime. Taking into consideration your relation with music, independence, and personal authenticity, identify how each of these themes may have impacted your own musical autobiography and sense of musicianship.

References

Allsup, R. (2016). *Remixing the classroom: Toward an open philosophy of music education*. Bloomington, IN: Indiana University Press.

Aloni, N. (2002). *Enhancing humanity: The philosophical foundations of humanistic education*. Dordrecht, Netherlands: Kulwer Academic Publishers.

Barry, C. T., Kerig, P. K., Stellwagen, K. K., & Garry, T. D. (2011). *Narcissism and machiavellianism in youth*. Washington, DC: American Psychological Association.

Brookfield, S. D. (2006). *The skillful teacher*. San Francisco, CA: Jossey-Bass.

Carey, B. (2015). *How we learn*. New York, NY: Random House.

Cranton, P. (2001). *Becoming an authentic teacher in higher education*. Malabar, FL: Krieger Publishing Company.

Coats, S. (2006). *Thinking as you play: Teaching piano in individual and group lessons*. Bloomington, IN: Indiana University Press.

Csikszentmihalyi, M. (1991). *Flow*. New York, NY: Harper & Row.

Cumming, N. (2000). *The sonic self*. Bloomington, IN: Indiana University Press.

Hotchkiss, S. (2002). *Why is always about you? The seven deadly sins of narcissism*. New York, NY: Free Press.

Jorgensen, E. R. (2008). *The art of teaching music*. Indianapolis, IN: Indiana University Press.

Kemp, A. E., & Mills, J. (2002). Musical potential. In R. Parncutt & G. E. McPherson (Eds.), *The science and psychology of music performance* (pp. 3–16). Oxford, UK: Oxford University Press.

Kivy, Peter. (2002). *Introduction to a philosophy of music*. Oxford, UK: Oxford University Press.

Kreber, C. (2013). *Authenticity in and through teaching*. Routledge.

Lasch, C. (1979). *The culture of narcissism*. New York: NY: Warner Books.

Niemi, H., Toom, A., & Kallioniemi, A. (2012). *Miracle of education: The principles and practices of teaching and learning in Finnish schools*. Rotterdam, Netherlands: Sense Publishers.

Nisbett, R. (2004). *The geography of thought*. New York, NY: Free Press.

Palmer, P. J. (1998). *The courage to teach*. San Francisco, CA: Jossey-Bass Publishers.

Pollei, P. (1991). Our evolving profession. *The Piano Quarterly, Spring, 153*, 54–55.

Rogers, C. (1969). *Freedom to learn*. Columbus, OH: Charles E. Merrill Publishing Company.

Schnabel, A. (1945/1961). *My life and music.* London, UK: Longmans.

Skalinder, B. (2016). *The music of teaching: Learning to trust students' natural development.* Milwaukee, WI: Hal Leonard Books.

Swinkin, J. (2015). *Teaching performance: A philosophy of piano pedagogy.* Dordrecht, Netherlands: Springer.

Taylor, C. (1991). *The ethics of authenticity.* Cambridge, MA: Harvard University Press.

Westney, W. (2003). *The perfect wrong note.* Pompton Plains, NJ: Amadeus Press.

Wolfe, T. (1976). The 'me' decade and the third great awakening. *New York Magazine,* August 23, 26–40.

Chapter 3
What Does Music Learning Look like?

Abstract In order to help teachers understand what happens when beginner piano students take their initial steps, this chapter examines the concept of learning from several relevant perspectives. Firstly, an overview of education theories indicates that learning is frequently interpreted as involving: (1) linear progressions, (2) making meaning from experience, (3) cyclical processes focused on exploration, and (4) the influence of individual and collective worldviews. Next, given the parallels between language learning and music learning, this chapter explores the process of language acquisition and transposes the principles of language learning to music learning. Finally, this chapter demonstrates how beginner piano students may move through three fundamental stages of musical development. The Background Stage involves how students informally acquire aspects of musicianship prior to formal lessons. The Foundation Stage focuses on tonalization development of technique and tone production as well as learning to play by ear. The Reading Stage continues to build on the Foundation Stage through the additional element of learning to read music.

When we learn, we take on, reinforce, or modify our own knowledge, behaviors, values, and skills. On certain occasions, we may learn intentionally, while on others, we may unintentionally learn something about ourselves or others. Learning may be goal oriented, may be internally and externally motivated. Learning is something we do under many kinds of circumstances—learning to play the piano being just one example. Yet, our understanding of what goes on when we learn or what's involved may be incomplete. So, it seems prudent to be purposeful in considering what's involved for beginner students learning to play the piano. In this chapter, I take a look at learning from several different perspectives including pertinent educational models of learning, language learning, learning to play by ear, and stages of learning to play the piano.

© The Author(s) 2018
M.B. Thompson, *Fundamentals of Piano Pedagogy*,
SpringerBriefs in Education, DOI 10.1007/978-3-319-65533-8_3

3.1 Models of Learning

Educational theorists, philosophers, and researchers have long debated the notion of learning within various cultural and historical frameworks. One model that has retained longevity is the depiction of learning as a linear process similar to the step-by-step way we might construct a building or assemble a car. Learning as a linear process has a certain kind of practicality to it, because under no circumstances could we learn everything at once. So, it seems appropriate to approach learning through sequences in which we move from one bit of information to the next or one part of a procedure to the next. Learning as a linear process tends to encourage automaticity or immediacy through deliberate and repetitious practice, focusing intentionally on mastery of each step before proceeding to the next.

In a second model, learning is depicted as the way we make sense of the world by relating new experiences to our own experiences and interpretations. Learning involves personal meaning making in which we're constantly putting things together, taking them apart, and reconfiguring how we think in an effort to maintain a coherent yet personally relevant picture of ourselves and the world around us. In learning as meaning making, we interpret the world complete with the messiness and discomfort associated with making mistakes. That's not to say that we only learn from experiences that disrupt our existing knowledge. Rather, it means that what we know of ourselves and the world is continually being affirmed, challenged, and updated by the breadth of new, familiar, interruptive, and affirmative personal experiences.

A third model with particular resonance in current educational theory portrays learning as a cyclical and explorative process more concerned with what's possible than what's predictable. Learning isn't merely accumulating more knowledge, more skills, more information, nor moving towards a pre-determined goal or destination. Learning is driven by our self-initiated desire to experiment, to try things out, and test what we already know or do in attempting to transform what we already know or do. In this creative and recursive model, learning contributes to the way we might evolve in terms of flourishing, maturity, deterioration, and irresponsibility. The underlying principle in exploring what's possible is that learning isn't about knowing where you're going, it's about finding out where you might get to.

A final model important to our understanding of learning has to do with the idea of nested forms. Nested forms is a term used by educational scholars Davis et al. (2015) to describe how learning integrates the biological, cognitive, social, cultural, and ecological dimensions of life. Learning doesn't take place as an isolated activity. Learning, as educator Jensen (1995) explained, "happens on many levels at once" (p. 18). It occurs as an integrated experience involving the simultaneous engagement of physical, emotional, interpersonal, auditory, and environmental themes even without our awareness. Notably, learning also has connections to spiritual dimensions including: relations with nature, anima mundi, faith in God, and indigenous belief systems. The guiding principle in this model is that learning draws not only from who we are, but also from our connection to life and the world around us. Learning isn't something that occurs only within the narrow confines of thinking about things. It's something that embodies and triggers an expansive overlapping that extends from the cellular to the behavioral, emotional to physical, scientific to spiritual, from the personal to the ecological—from each of us, to all of us, to life, and to the world.

Looking at learning thusly, we see that learning isn't defined by a singular course of acquiring knowledge, skills, or understanding. Learning arises within and in response to the diverse opportunities of everyday life. While an extensive inquiry into learning would undoubtedly reveal further depictions, this brief examination indicates that learning is an adaptive process shaped by the natural interplay of various overlapping dynamics. Learning involves the potential integration of linear learning structures, individual meaning making, cyclical processes of experimentation, and the influence of personal and collective worldviews.

3.2 Language Learning

One of the most common ways music educators have interpreted music learning is through its parallels with language learning. As music educators Gellrich and Sundin (1993) indicated, learning music is "very similar to the acquisition of a child's first language" (p. 141). For children, language learning is something they accomplish in stages that begin with babbling, followed by learning to speak actual words, and subsequently learning to read.

Language learning occurs because children are surrounded by spoken language and because they have something to say. Children as young as four months of age demonstrate distinct preferences for speech patterns typical of their own language. They respond to and select sounds that have meaning. Before speaking words, children begin with babbling, a period of experimenting with making sounds and imitating the rhythmic characteristics of speaking their language (MacWhinney 2001, p. 469). Gradually, they learn to speak, using experimentation and imitation to progress from one- or two-word sentences to joined sentences. They learn to recognize and reproduce sound patterns and meanings as essential to their becoming members of a language and social community (Bruning et al. 1999). Learning to speak doesn't really start by prescribing the sounds children are allowed to make. Language learning begins with explorations in which children connect the sounds they're trying to make with what they hear, with what they want to communicate. They develop their own auditory sensitivity, distinguishing one kind of sound from another as well as producing one sound instead of another with nuance and precision. They create their own physical or technical competency, experiencing how breathing and moving their tongues, lips, and mouths may change the sounds they're making.

Subsequent to their learning to speak, children may broaden their language learning by learning to read written words. What's important in this stage is that children learn to read by connecting the words they already speak with the symbols that represent them (Bruning et al. 1999). However, the purpose of learning to read is more than simply matching visual clues with spoken vocabulary. Similar to learning to speak, learning to read has value as a matter of personal communication and meaning making. Reading expands language fluency by introducing new contexts, thoughts, and ideas that may confirm, expand, and challenge how people envision the world around them.

Language learning operates through recursive cycles in which exploration, experimentation, and imitation stimulate the development of auditory sensitivity, physical coordination, and visual perception, and vice versa. Yet, these cycles also depend on active participation or meaningful involvement to prompt exploration and development. Active participation keeps learning in motion. Through this process, children foster ownership of what language means and represents. This means that language learning is neither a distant nor passive process. Language learning occurs as something meaningful, as something personally relevant that children actively accomplish in fulfillment of their desire to communicate.

From this broad example of language learning, several points stand out as important for learning to play the piano. Firstly and above all else, meaningful music learning depends on students' genuine participation. When students are meaningfully involved in music learning, they actively connect with various aspects of their musical explorations—it's fun, it feels right, it may be hard but it works. They take ownership of their own learning, no matter where it leads them. In contrast, students who aren't meaningfully involved may have limited or nonexistent connections to their music learning—it's not fun, it's a requirement, it's temporary. They may surrender ownership of their learning, choosing instead to continue as passive, obedient, or compliant participants. Meaningful participation means that music learning is something students not only enjoy, it's something they take pride in doing for themselves.

Secondly, children begin language learning by experimenting with and imitating the characteristic sounds of their spoken language. Similarly for music learning, making sound takes priority as the foundation for music learning. This idea is reflected in students' learning by ear explorations of tone production and physical coordination as the first learning step. This idea of experimentation and its relationship with imitation also has implications for a third point.

Thirdly, what's interesting about experimentation and imitation is how these explorative tools operate as back up plans for each other. For example, when students have in mind a particular musical element—technical, rhythmic, melodic, harmonic, interpretative—they may use either experimentation or imitation to get closer. When experimenting doesn't work, they can try imitating their teacher, a recording, or another performer. And conversely, when imitation doesn't work, they may experiment with any number of emotional, physical, intuitive, or spiritual variations. However, musical experimentation and imitation have benefits and drawbacks. Experimentation is especially valuable when there's no immediate model at hand, yet it loses value when fatigue or frustration sets in. While under all circumstances, the value of imitation is completely reliant on meaningful student involvement.

A fourth point takes into consideration the fundamental connection between auditory sensitivity and physical coordination. In language learning, children's ability to distinguish sounds provides the vital link for how they produce sounds. Similarly in music learning, listening and performing are intimately connected. There's a reciprocal relationship between the sounds students hear or anticipate hearing and what they do to make those sounds. While listening and performing may be approached as separate musical aspects, their inter-relationship reveals that each may be experienced in the other. In other words, listening is reflected in students' performance—both as input and output; and performance relies on what students hear—also both in terms of input and output. And, because listening and performing take place on many levels at once, their back-and-forth relationship encompasses the possibility of imaginative, physical, auditory, emotional, inter-personal, and spiritual dimensions.

Finally, music learning is an "ear-before-eye" process, similar to the way in which language learning proceeds from speaking to reading. When students begin music reading, they connect what they play by ear with the symbols that represent what they're playing. This means that students' initial music reading experiences are more about reading what they already know how to play, than about perpetu-ating interval recognition and the mathematical relationships of note values. Learning to play by ear provides the much-needed auditory context for learning to read music, while music reading is essential to the ongoing expansion and evolution of fluent musical performance.

3.3 Learning to Play by Ear

Prominent educators and musicians throughout history have consistently advocated learning to play by ear as the first step in music learning. Educational principles developed by the Swiss educator Pestalozzi (1746–1827) are particularly relevant. Pestalozzi believed that direct experience was the basis of all education and the purpose of education was to develop the whole person. Learning, according to Pestalozzi, proceeded by moving from the "known to the unknown" (Schleuter 1997, p. 21). Although Pestalozzi never taught music, European and North American music teachers have applied his ideas. Mason (1792–1872), an esteemed American musician who taught in Boston during the early 1800s, is just one of many music teachers who acknowledge Pestalozzi's educational ideas in the emphasis on "sounds before signs" (McPherson and Gabrielsson 2002, p. 101).

Moving to the twentieth century, the idea of "sounds before signs" learning has taken on various descriptors including ear-before-eye, learning by ear, sound to symbol, and playing by ear. The Suzuki Method has been a strong voice in advocating ear-before-eye learning through a Mother Tongue approach—the idea that children learn to speak before they learn to read. While Founder of the Suzuki Method, Suzuki (1969) based the Mother Tongue Theory on his casual observation of children, formal research from music educators around the globe has affirmed the value of ear-before-eye learning. In Great Britain, music educator Mainwaring (1951) was among the first researchers to study the acquisition of ear-before-eye playing skills. For Mainwaring, the most natural way of learning to play a musical instrument is by proceeding "from sound to symbol, not from symbol to sound" (p. 12). As another British music researcher Sloboda (1978) explained, the rationale of an ear-before-eye approach is that "without some musical knowledge a beginner has no expectancies which can be used in reading" (p. 15). In the United States, Gordon (1971) affirmed that hearing music and playing by ear form the necessary readiness for every other level of musical learning. "Because music is an aural art, one must first acquire aural perception and kinesthetic reaction in order to develop musical understanding in a conceptual sense... That is, 'sound' must be taught before 'sign' can be given meaning" (p. 61). In a similar vein, results of a three-year longitudinal study of 101 instrumentalists by music education scholar Gary McPherson also confirmed that "playing by ear helps student musicians learn to coordinate ear, eye, and hand and to perform on their instrument what they see in notation and hear or imagine in their mind" (McPherson et al. 1997, p. 126). Based on the above researchers' observations, music learning clearly has its anchor in our auditory relationships with music.

3.4   Learning to Play the Piano

Thus far, this chapter has examined multiple perspectives relevant to the process of learning to play the piano. Four models of learning shed light on linear learning, meaning making, cyclical experimentations, and the nested influence of personal and collective worldviews. Investigation into language learning revealed "ear-before-eye" learning processes involving experimentation and imitation, auditory sensitivity, physical coordination, visual perception, and active participation through meaningful involvement.

According to our investigation, learning to play the piano brings together an interweaving of *structure, development,* and *meaning.*[1] As a linear sequence, music learning may use a structure that begins with learning by ear and subsequently involves learning through reading. Music learning stimulates development through experimentation and imitation in the areas of auditory sensitivity, physical coordination, and visual perception. Development also involves the exploration of possibilities. In addition, music learning relies on the meaning students derive from their active participation and the nested influence of personal and collective worldviews.

The challenge is that children and adults may have different and slightly incompatible interpretations of structure, development, and meaning. Whereas

---

[1] I use the term *meaning* in reference to the individual ways students may interpret or make sense of their music lessons and the various aspects involved in learning to play a musical instrument. *Meaning* is also concerned with what's behind students' active participation in terms of the diverse reasons that may support their own meaningful involvement.

adults may respond to structure as a matter requiring personal discipline or responsibility, children may understand structure as primarily involving play. Part of what makes play valuable as a mode of learning for children is that it lowers the emotional stakes of failure (Jenkins 2009, p. 38). It allows them to take risks and learn through trial and error. For adults, structure may indicate the need for planning and control, while children may view structure as something that spontaneously unfolds.

Music educator Gordon (1993) provides a noteworthy insight into development, in that adults emphasize quality whereas children may focus on quantity. Adult attitudes towards development may be selective in comparison to children who may absorb whatever the environment has to offer. Development as a matter of quantity often shows up in children's desire to play fast and loud—a development most adults consider as noisy interruption.

Finally, the meaning adults attribute to music learning may differ from children, wherein adults may create hierarchies of value associated with certain musical achievements like performing with no mistakes or intentional results. In contrast, children may be less discriminating of their musical experiences that range from satisfying involvement to complete distraction. This is not to say that performances without mistakes are equal in value to distracted musical wanderings. However, it's easy to see how an exclusive no-mistakes mindset might inadvertently generate a fear of making mistakes or trying something new, as well as unintentionally stifling imagination and creativity. Additionally, children may make meaning as a matter of immediacy rather than the delayed gratification approach of adults.

This means that structure, development, and meaning aren't so much the hard and fast rules of music learning. Learning to play the piano isn't about deciding whether children's or adults' attitudes and insights should lead the way. Structure, development, and meaning are more about providing a framework for what Davis (2004) referred to as "opening up new spaces of possibility by exploring current spaces" (p. 184). They act as reminders for both where we are and where we might consider going. So, with this in mind and with the understanding that music learning involves exploring what we know in order to uncover what we have yet to imagine, the following linear sequence takes into consideration the results of our exploration into music learning thus far:

- Background stage—individual musical experiences
- Foundation stage—tone production, physical coordination, learning by ear, tonality
- Reading stage—vocabulary, sound to symbol, learning by reading.

3.4.1 Background Stage

Even before children begin formal music lessons, structure, development, and meaning show up in their background experiences. There's a structure of play in their dabbling with instruments and learning through auditory experiences. Using experimentation and imitation, children develop their own informal yet amazing musical applications. And, there's meaning in the way students draw from their individual experiences with music and create their own personal ways of making sense of music.

Music is something students get to know through ordinary everyday encounters in their families, with friends, on TV, on the computer, and in their communities. Children demonstrate their ability to make sense of their musical experiences in a number of ways. For example, children are able to remember musical selections and distinguish one musical example from another. When asked to recall music they've just heard, they can make plausible approximations. They can recognize harmonic textures in terms of discordant inconsistencies within a musical selection. And, they can identify the mood or emotional intent of a musical passage (Sloboda 1993). Children learn about music simply by living in their cultural environment, and the musical grammar they develop is a direct result of the sounds that come into their ears. As Campbell (2006) has affirmed, children "sing because they must, they move because the music prompts them, and they dabble with instruments and sound sources out of curiosity, a need for tactile experience, and because it 'feels good' to do so" (p. 433).

> *Noah's Background Story*—At five years of age, Noah is the second child in his family to learn to play the piano. He's already learned to sing songs at daycare, in church, and at home. Recently, he attended his older brother Patrick's piano lesson. After Patrick's lesson was finished, Noah jumped on the piano bench and proceeded to plunk out various portions from Patrick's pieces. Soon after, Noah started lessons of his own.
> *Bella's Background Story*—Bella is the only child in her family. She knows how to sing many songs from school, movies, and TV. She also likes to dance, but not in any formal kind of way. At a birthday party, her friend Erica played some pieces on the piano. Soon after, Bella started tentatively depressing the keys on her piano at home.

3.4.2 Foundation Stage

Structure in the Foundation Stage of learning to play the piano consists of a linear progression involving: (1) tonalization exercises, (2) right hand and left hand melodies, and (3) right hand melodies with left hand accompaniment. Development focuses on a composite of tone production, physical coordination, listening awareness, and learning to play by ear. Meaning involves a spectrum of explorations from specific goals to playing around to making music (see Chap. 2—our relation with music).

Similar to the way children's language learning involves manipulating the sounds and rhythmic characteristics of their spoken language, learning to play the piano begins by developing students' fluency in tone production and physical coordination. Music education scholar Schleuter (1997) has affirmed the importance of beginning with tone production, "Musical sound and tone quality are always emphasized first. The student's goal is to produce familiar musical sounds" (p. 125). In the 1930s, violinist Shinichi Suzuki introduced tone production as the fundamental starting point for music learning (Suzuki 1969). More recently, music education scholars Duke and Byo (2011) proposed developing "beautiful tone" as essential to students' very first experiences of music learning (p. 5). One advantage is that students may develop listening and performing skills without the distraction of reading notation. Because students may have difficulty learning more than one thing at a time, beginning with tone production allows students to wholly focus on the listening and performing skills needed to produce good tone.

As the overarching focus in the Foundation Stage, tone production involves students' fluency in producing expressive sounds reflective of the instrument's resonant potential and their own personal attributes. Piano students start with tonalization exercises that facilitate right hand and left hand skills of producing tone. With a focus on tone and technique, tonalization exercises may use a "theme and variations" type model that facilitates student development of tonal and technical fluency. Examples of tonalization "themes" may include melodies such as *Hot Cross Buns*, Queen's *We Will Rock You*, and *Mary had a Little Lamb*. Tonalization exercises "variations" develop legato and non-legato tone qualities (and combinations thereof) in each hand through exploration of rhythmic patterns. What's important is that tonalization exercises incorporate repetition of a relevant tonal/technical aspect and that individual tonalizations may be broken down into smaller units and expanded to larger units as appropriate to students' development. Teachers may use small amounts of rote teaching to assist students in learning tonalization exercises notes and fingerings. Following adequate mastery of tonalization, students may progress to right hand and left hand melodies.[2]

Right hand and left hand melodies facilitate further development of tone production and physical coordination skills by reinforcing students' comfort with basic 5-finger melodies and gradually exploring melodies that gently move out of 5-finger positioning. Students learn these melodies by ear through listening to CDs or video recordings similar to the way they learn to speak their surrounding spoken language. Listening to repertoire recordings helps students become familiar with pieces before they play them and avoid getting completely off track with their own personal distortions or exaggerations once they've learned a particular piece. However, the most important outcome of this aspect is that students acquire a sense of

---

[2]At a workshop I facilitated for all instruments studio music teachers, wind instrument teachers indicated their preference for beginning with 3-note and 5-note scale passages as tonalization exercises. String teachers emphasized the importance of beginning with open string tonalization exercises.

tonality. Students get familiar with where pitches are located on their instrument and a sense that pitches have unchanging relations with each other.

When piano students progress to hands together melody and accompaniment repertoire, the focus on tone production and physical coordination continues. Teachers may assist with small amounts of rote teaching and Playback Games to help students gain familiarity with basic chord accompaniment patterns. Through adequate listening to the repertoire CD, students gain understanding of chord progressions, in particular the way chords function in relation to the melody. In this view, learning to play hands together not only reinforces tone development and physical ease, but also nurtures students' ability to recognize harmonic textures within a musical selection. Students experience for themselves what it means to assemble the melody and accompaniment of a musical selection.

Through the Foundation Stage structure of tonalization exercises, right hand and left hand melodies, and hands together melodies and accompaniments, students experience what it means to produce, listen for, and evaluate their own tone production. They learn how their own personal involvement—body posture, intentionality, breathing, hand position, fingers and arms, attitude, gestures and motions—affects the sounds they produce. They also develop the ability to learn by ear, discovering that their instrument isn't an impenetrable field of unknown pitches; the piano is intimately connected to the music they already hear inside their own heads.

Finally, in this Foundation Stage of learning, there's a word of caution regarding rote teaching—a process in which students copy various aspects of the teacher's performance model including: notes and rhythms, fingerings, hand position and body posture, and desired qualities of tone. While rote teaching has its obvious merits in terms of assisting students in learning repertoire, an over-subscription to rote teaching may be detrimental. Students may miss out on the benefits of listening to their repertoire CD and their own experimentations. Excessive rote teaching may overtake the benefits of students' natural learning progression involving recognizing mistakes and figuring how to actually learn by ear. Rote teaching has immense value in terms of acquiring certain repertoire details and noticeable disadvantages for students' proficiency in learning the repertoire by ear.

David's Foundation Story—During his first few months of piano lessons, I helped six-year-old David work through four non-legato and legato tonalization exercises. I used Suzuki's "Twinkle Theme & Variations" because each tonalization exercise follows identical fingerings and notes. To facilitate David's learning at his first lesson, I broke down the first tonalization into small chunks I could teach by rote. With a few weeks' practice, David could perform the first right hand tonalization with adequate tone, good notes and fingerings. So, I helped him start the first left hand tonalization, making sure he incorporated appropriate left hand fingerings (David already knew the appropriate notes from his right hand tonalization). As each tonalization became more secure, I used minimal amounts of rote teaching to introduce the non-legato and legato aspects of subsequent tonalization exercises. By the end of his second month, David's tone production and physical coordination were sufficiently secure, signaling his readiness for right hand melodies.

Listening to his repertoire CD and performing his tonalization exercises gave David the sense of where notes are located on the piano necessary for him to learn melodies by ear. To ensure his independent success in melody learning, I always made sure David could find the melody's first note with an appropriate fingering, knowing that he might never master "Mary Had a Little Lamb" if he started with right hand thumb on C. Singing the melodies with words helped him get familiar with entire pieces. When David could fluently play five right hand melodies and two left hand melodies (hands separately), along with his tonalization exercises, he seemed sufficiently secure in terms of tone production, physical coordination, and learning by ear to begin hands together pieces.

After teaching David the left hand C and G chords for "Mary Had a Little Lamb", I asked him to play/experiment with the left hand chords while I played the melody. Similar to David's experience in learning melodies by ear, listening to his repertoire CD gave him the sense of where the chords needed to be played. At home, David successfully completed "Mary Had a Little Lamb" hands together. As David become more comfortable with "Mary" hands together, I introduced a Playback Game to help him get familiar with Alberti bass patterns CGEG and BGDG. This game involved covering my own hand with a sheet of paper to obscure David's view, playing various left hand combinations (CCC, GGG, CDEFG, GFEDC, CGC before trying CGEG & BGDG), and David playing back the combinations. Using CGEG and BGDG, I asked David to play/experiment with the left hand patterns while I played the "Lightly Row" melody. At home, David successfully completed "Lightly Row" hands together. Listening to the repertoire CD made it easy for him, because as he said, "I can hear the left hand in my head."

David completed his Foundation Stage tonalization exercises and a total of 16 Foundation Stage pieces during a one-year period. Throughout that time, I repeatedly used the above strategy of learning the right hand melody by ear, using Playbacks to get familiar with left hand patterns, and continuing to reinforce tone production and physical coordination throughout David's progressive journey.

3.4.3 Reading Stage

In keeping with the framework of structure, development, and meaning, the Reading Stage structure involves: (1) reading what students already know how to play, (2) reading "Music Reading Books", and (3) reading new repertoire. Development builds on the Foundation Stage vocabulary, keyboard geography, and visual symbols to promote connections between learning by ear and learning by reading. Development also continues to build tone production, physical coordination, and listening awareness. Similar to the Foundation Stage, meaning involves a spectrum of explorations from specific goals to playing around to making music (Chap. 2—our relation with music).

To understand what's involved in learning to read music, it may be advantageous to examine the parallel process in learning to read words. At a most basic level, children learn to read words through a step-by-step process. Once they have fluency in speaking their language, learning to read involves: (1) memorizing the alphabet, (2) learning to visually recognize the printed alphabet, (3) connecting spoken sounds with the letters of the alphabet, and (4) transforming printed words into combinations of sounds. In their early stages as readers, children learn to read words they already know. They use only a limited portion of the alphabet in reading simple words that are part of their spoken vocabulary. Some three- to five-year-old children learn to read familiar words like picking out their name on a birthday card or identifying the logo of a recognizable location such as a restaurant name. Over time, children gradually acquire skills of rapid decoding that eventually become automatic processing necessary for reading effectively and accurately (Bruning et al. 1999).

Following the example of learning to read words, students may learn to read music using a step-by-step process that starts with various practices leading up to music reading. In the Foundation Stage, teachers sow the seeds of music reading as a matter of practical communication from the outset. For example, students learn how note names—A, B, C, D, E, F, G—refer to particular pitches and designated places on the keyboard, or how the term treble clef makes reference to high-pitched notes, or how the words legato and staccato describe specific types of tone. Their musical vocabulary is grounded in the experiences of listening and performing.

When students' listening, performing, and musical vocabulary are comfortably established in the Foundation Stage, teachers may sow another seed associated with music reading. They help students get familiar with the visual music notation that represents the sounds they play. For example, students learn how the notes they play—A, B, C, D, E, F, G—are represented on a five line staff, how the sounds of legato and staccato are indicated in a musical score, how the quarter notes they play look different from half notes. Students connect the individual letters/notes and signs of music notation with their corresponding sounds, similar to the language learning experience of connecting letters of the alphabet to specific spoken sounds. They learn how music notation represents individual aspects of sound and specific places on the keyboard. With fluency in terms of their musical vocabulary and a basic introduction to music notation by the end of the Foundation Stage, students may be ready to begin formal music reading.

According to music education scholars McPherson and Gabrielsson (2002), the most advantageous way for students to learn music reading is by reading repertoire they already know how to play. This process resembles the way children learn to read their language by reading words they already know and by reading printed words as combinations of sounds rather than individual letters. Here, students generate musical units or groupings from music notation in contrast to the Foundation Stage recognition of individual letters/notes and signs. They read music notation as units of sound. An immediate problem with reading already learned repertoire is that once students have read the first bar of an already learned piece, there may be no incentive to continue reading because they know the piece from memory. So, it's not entirely productive for students to read repertoire they've already learned.

A possible solution for reading students' already learned repertoire involves the practice of scrambles—a simple reading exercise that deconstructs a four-bar phrase into individual bars and repositions the bars in a scrambled order. This means that students read scrambled four-bar phrases of material they already know, but have never seen in this particular scrambled context. The benefits of scrambles are enormous because students experience music reading as a matter of musical units or groupings. They learn to read music as the experience of confidently knowing what musical units sound like.[3]

Learning new repertoire also has importance for learning to read music. With their initial experience of having learned repertoire by ear in the Foundation Stage, students are equipped to subsequently augment their repertoire learning strategies with music reading. While students fluent in learning repertoire by ear will undoubtedly continue to benefit from listening to repertoire recordings, music reading has several practical values. Firstly, when students have difficulty figuring out a certain pitch or rhythmic pattern by ear, reading the music may help clarify individual notes or rhythms. Secondly, music reading permits students to refine select portions of pieces without starting at the beginning. Students may attend to specific details and passages unachievable through learning by ear. Thirdly, reading the new repertoire means that students' music reading skills keep pace with their musical development, therein contributing to their success and satisfaction as musicians.

Jasmine's Reading Story—Beginning in the Foundation Stage, six-year-old Jasmine gradually got comfortable with the note names (A, B, C, etc.) through various note-name-based activities I introduced such as: "Find all the Cs", "Show me the first note of Twinkle. What's its name?" "Which piece starts on G?" "Let's say the note names going up (and down)". Midway through the Foundation Stage, I used flash cards to help her get visually

---

[3]For an example of a scrambles-based reading methodology, please see the forthcoming publication: Thompson, M.B. *PLAY & READ*.

familiar with notes in the treble and bass clefs. I asked Jasmine to tell me "What's this note's name?" as well as show me "Where is it on the piano?" and "What does it sound like?" I also helped her get familiar with simple rhythmic notation through recognizing and clapping.

Following completion of the Foundation Stage, Jasmine's formal reading development included two long-term activities: (1) Reading scrambles as the precursor to "Music Reading Books", and (2) Reading her new repertoire. Firstly, reading scrambles involved reading the scrambled versions of 4-bar phrases Jasmine already knew how to play. Each week, Jasmine worked on two pages of scrambles from a single piece with a different focus: writing note names and finger numbers, clapping with the beat, identifying one-bar units of notes, singing the scrambles, playing the scrambles, and writing her own scrambles. Over a period of six months, the reading scrambles process helped Jasmine get familiar with hearing the score and feeling the rhythms before she played them. Subsequent to this activity, Jasmine gradually progressed through a number of "Music Reading Books" continuing the same holistic process of writing, singing, playing, hearing the notes, and feeling the rhythms.

Secondly, Jasmine's music reading development involved reading her new repertoire and building purposely on her Foundation Stage skill of learning to play by ear. By listening to her repertoire CD, Jasmine always had a basic sense of each new piece in her ear. To handle the increasing difficulty in each new piece, I encouraged Jasmine to actively utilize the score as her most practical learning resource. Initially, Jasmine meticulously wrote in the note names and finger numbers for every single note in a piece. Whenever she struggled with note names, fingering, or rhythms, I'd help her to write in an appropriate solution. Writing in this information meant that Jasmine could confidently learn her new repertoire on her own. She could also practise hands separately and practise specific bars that needed extra work. She had all the information she needed—learning by ear and by reading—to practise independently. Of course, Jasmine sometimes showed up with errors in her reading. Rather than interpret her errors as a sign of incompetence, I used her misreading as opportunity to clarify the details of music reading. Interestingly, Jasmine continued to write note names and finger numbers in her repertoire pieces for about a year. Then, over the period of a few months, I suggested she gradually reduce her reliance on writing. Two years later, Jasmine had very little reliance on writing and only wrote in the information she considered to be absolutely necessary much like any professional musician. Currently, eleven-year-old Jasmine reads a variety of music from pop music to duets to guitar chord sheets and her formal classical repertoire.

3.5 Growth and Rest

My goal in this chapter has been to shed light on what happens when students take their initial steps in learning to play the piano. Through a sequence of Background, Foundation, and Reading Stages that fulfill overlapping and distinct purposes, these stages sometimes act as reminders for where we are. At other times, they remind us about where we might consider going. Yet, having looked at music learning from various perspectives, a final thought remains. It's the idea that music learning involves a cyclical pattern of growth and rest, wherein teachers acknowledge that some days are better suited to growth and other days are more about rest. There's an interdependent relationship between growth and rest, just like in our ordinary daily lives. Periods of growth necessitate periods of rest. When students have the time to rest their body, mind, and soul, it means they'll soon be ready for growth. With this final observation, it seems appropriate to describe music learning as a reflection of everyday life—one that inescapably and fortunately involves the ever returning exchanges of joyful celebrations, unanticipated setbacks, and welcome rejuvenation.

3.6 Before We Move on

1. What does this chapter's description of language learning have in common with your own development as a musician? What similarities do you notice between your experience of learning to play a musical instrument (or sing) and language learning's emphasis on the surrounding environment and learning by ear?
2. With the understanding that music learning may begin with Background Stage, describe as fully as possible your own development prior to beginning formal music lessons? What events and people were most influential?
3. The Foundation Stage of music learning emphasizes beginning with tone production and technique. What are the benefits and disadvantages of this approach? How does this stage of tonalization compare to your own autobiographical experiences related to tone production and technique?
4. Music education researchers have frequently proposed that music lessons begin with students learning to play by ear. Yet, a majority of current student method books perpetuate the tradition of learning by reading. Why do you think publishing companies continue to produce music reading methodologies when research indicates learning to play by ear processes may be more in sync with beginner music students?

5. The Reading Stage of music learning describes how students' first efforts in learning to read may involve reading repertoire they already know how to play. What similarities and differences with this approach to music reading do you see in your own musical development?
6. How does this chapter reinforce your music teaching? What might you want to adjust in your teaching?

References

Bruning, R., Schraw, G., & Ronning, R. (1999). *Cognitive psychology and instruction* (3rd ed.). Columbus, OH: Merrill.

Campbell, P. S. (2006). Global practices. In G. McPherson (Ed.), *The child as musician* (pp. 415–438). Oxford, UK: Oxford University Press.

Davis, B. (2004). *Inventions of teaching*. New York, NY: Laurence Erbaum Associates.

Davis, B., Sumara, D., & Luce-Kapler, R. (2015). *Engaging minds* (3rd ed.). New York, NY: Routledge.

Duke, R., & Byo, J. (2011). *The habits of musicianship*. Louisiana State University.

Gellrich, M., & Sundin, B. (1993). Instrumental practice in the 18th and 19th centuries. *Council for Research in Music Education, 119,* 137–145.

Gordon, E. (1993). *Learning sequences in music*. Chicago, IL: GIA Publications.

Gordon, E. (1971). *The psychology of music teaching*. Englewood Cliffs, NJ: Prentice-Hall.

Jenkins, H. (2009). *Confronting the challenges of participatory culture*. Cambridge, MA: MIT Press.

Jensen, E. (1995). *Super teaching*. San Diego, CA: The Brain Store.

Mainwaring, J. (1951). *Teaching music in schools*. London, UK: Paxton.

MacWhinney, B. (2001). First language acquisition. In M. Aronoff & J. Rees-Miller (Eds.), *The handbook of Linguistics*. Malden, MA: Blackwell.

McPherson, G. E., & Gabrielsson, A. (2002). From sound to sign. In R. Parncutt & G. McPherson (Eds.), *The science and psychology of music performance* (pp. 99–115). Oxford, UK: Oxford University Press.

McPherson, G., Bailey, M., & Sinclair, K. (1997). Path analysis of a model to describe the relationship between five types of musical performance. *Journal of Research in Music Education, 45*(1), 103–129.

Schleuter, S. L. (1997). *A sound approach to teaching instrumentalists*. New York, NY: Schirmer Books.

Sloboda, J. (1993). Musical ability. In G. R. Brock & K. Ackrill (Eds.), *The origins and development of high ability* (pp. 106–118). Chichester, UK: Wiley.

Sloboda, J. (1978). The psychology of music reading. *Psychology of Music, 6*(2), 3–20.

Suzuki, S. (1969). *Nurtured by love*. Hicksville, NY: Exposition Press Inc.

Chapter 4
What Does Teaching the Piano Look like?

Abstract Teaching beginner piano students is an endeavor that builds implicitly and explicitly on teachers' beliefs, musical ideals, and personal values. This chapter begins by exploring how many twenty-first century teaching resources and practices have their origins in the piano's history, influential educational movements, as well as scientific and industrial developments of the 1800s. As alternatives to this pedagogic history, teachers may incorporate principles of democracy and parenting as models for instruction—two approaches that highlight how teaching is concerned with the relationships between teachers and students. Democratic music teachers draw from the ideals of freedom, equality, and dignity to solicit their students' thoughts and opinions. Democratic teaching emphasizes how the teacher's role has inherently moral and ethical undertones. The parenting model highlights how teachers begin by leading because students may not know the way, they hand over the musical tools students need for successful mastery, and they expand students' ongoing mastery of musicianship.

When we consider the process of teaching, many interpretations come to mind because teaching is a practice embedded in centuries of tradition, philosophy, ideologies, and social practices. As a consequence, today, we connect teaching with numerous synonyms and descriptive metaphors—

Teaching as "instructing"	Teaching as "training"
Teaching as "nurturing"	Teaching as "mentoring"
Teaching as "enlightening"	Teaching as "indoctrinating"

These synonyms and metaphors shed light on various perspectives of piano teaching. On occasion, piano teaching is all about showing or leading the way. On others, it's about empowering. At times, piano teachers (as well as their vocal and instrumental colleagues) endeavor to draw out the student. Yet, this collection of synonyms and metaphors doesn't really tell us why music teachers teach the way they do. Or, in particular, why piano teachers might approach teaching in a certain way.

M.B. Thompson, *Fundamentals of Piano Pedagogy*,
SpringerBriefs in Education, DOI 10.1007/978-3-319-65533-8_4

This chapter turns to the immediate historical past to examine the roots of our current approach to studio music teaching. It explores how piano teaching has a lot to do with the piano's history, influential educational movements, as well as scientific and industrial developments. As an alternative to traditional authoritarian music teaching models, this chapter draws from music education scholars Allsup (2007) and De Lorenzo (2003) to consider the ideals of democratic teaching relationships involving liberty, equality, and human dignity. This chapter also proposes the example of parenting as a model of instruction wherein teachers play a vital role in leading, handing over, and expanding the diverse layers of students' musical development.

4.1 Piano Teaching from a Historical Perspective

Prior to the 1850s, musicianship was primarily regarded as a craft passed from one generation to the next through a musical apprenticeship. The goal of teaching keyboard instruments like the harpsichord or clavichord was to develop versatile musicians comfortable with performance, improvisation, composition, and conducting. In keeping with the traditions that had served centuries of musicians, musical masters encouraged their students to reproduce the rules handed down from previous masters, elaborate on the masters, and invent their own pieces. Keyboard music teachers often taught their beginner students on a daily basis, blurring the separation between lessons and practice, and purposefully helping students settle into the routine of making music. Inventing pieces was time consuming but necessary as printed musical scores were rare and expensive. Students studied their teacher's compositions as a source for their own inventions, and copying and composing music played an important role (Gellrich and Sundin 1993).

For keyboard instructors during the 1700s and 1800s, the evolution of musical styles brought changes to music teaching. The fuller resonance of orchestral music no longer required the harpsichord as part of its texture, and solo piano repertoire assumed a prestige that solo harpsichord or clavichord literature had never achieved. Piano performance took on a cultural status equal to that of composing or conducting. Teaching the piano moved away from the versatility of a musical apprenticeship because playing the piano was interpreted as an activity in itself, rather than part of or means to the broader achievement of musicianship. While the noticeable evolution of musical styles occurred as a result of aesthetic, cultural, and personal expressions, changes related to the Scientific and Industrial Revolutions in addition to educational developments of the 1800s also have significance for a historical understanding of music teaching.

One development from the Industrial Revolution with a surprising influence on studio music teaching occurred in 1818—the invention of the lithograph and high speed printing machines. By 1830, publishing companies were able to mass-produce relatively inexpensive musical scores in large quantities (McPherson and Gabrielsson 2002). Whereas the previous generation of musicians had limited printed resources, easy access to printed materials effectively brought an end to the tradition of a comprehensive musical apprenticeship. As a result, the nature of music teaching shifted its emphasis from music as a creative art involving impro- visation and composition, to an emphasis on music as a reproductive art that focused on technique and interpretation. Keyboard composers like Clementi (1752– 1832), Cramer (1771–1858), Czerny (1791–1857), and Hanon (1819–1900) pub- lished numerous volumes of exercises and studies as the cornerstones of piano teaching. Piano methods and teachers of the nineteenth century were, in large part, concerned with technique (Uszler et al. 1991, p. 113). An unfortunate consequence was that repetitious practice of technical musical exercises replaced the spontaneity and creativity associated with the apprenticeship model. So, while greater access to printed musical scores meant music teachers and their students could connect with a broader musical repertoire, the pervasiveness of printed technical exercises meant students frequently practiced for long hours to develop specific skills that had limited practical application in performing the repertoire.

An educational development during the 1800s with relevance to music instruction was the emergence of compulsory public schooling. With the goal of efficiently providing education for all citizens, public schooling moved quickly to implement instructional processes highly reminiscent of an industrial assembly line. All subject matters, including the fine arts, were deconstructed and linearized, allowing for uniformity of delivery and mastery. Students' learning process focused on rote repetition of routinized procedures—a "drill and kill" educational approach that incorporated excessive duplication of isolated skills without regard for stu- dents' holistic understanding of the subject. Teachers were tasked with controlling students' progress or lack thereof, much like supervisors in a factory. Indeed, the entire school building and its classrooms were constructed in a manner that facil- itated teachers' watchful surveillance and authoritative control at all times (Davis 2004). Compulsory public schooling functioned as the logical, carefully planned progression through isolated aspects of subject matters in which grading and exams provide the measurement of successful learning. With evident links between edu- cational developments and the prevailing scientific and industrial models of the 1800s, it's interesting to note how the deconstruction of subjects, teacher control, systematization of isolated skills, rote repetition, and graded learning would show up as staples of the conservatory approach to music instruction.

The notion of a conservatory wherein aspiring musicians devote years to refining their musical skills dates back to Italy in the 1500s. During the early 1800s, many conservatories were founded in central Europe, but it was the establishment of the Leipzig Conservatory in 1843 that provided the catalyst for an explosion of such institutions in German-speaking countries (Parakilas 1999). Under the direction of composer Mendelssohn (1809–1847), Leipzig Conservatory students participated in a three-year curriculum that balanced theory with practice—the goal being to acquire a well-rounded musical education similar to the previous generations' musical apprenticeship model. However, Mendelssohn's influence was cut short by his untimely death, and the ideal of a balanced curriculum was quickly abandoned in favor of a systematized curriculum focused on virtuosity. Music teachers closely monitored their students' technical development, requiring students to learn pieces from a standardized repertoire list and participate in annual performance examinations. By the latter half of the 1800s, the Leipzig Conservatory and those schools modeled after it became known as virtuoso factories, reflective of the systematic approach that emphasized drill and uniformity at the expense of imagination and individuality. While many students obviously achieved a high level of artistry and musicianship through a conservatory approach to music instruction, others found it boring and uninspiring.

Looking at these various historical developments, it's easy to see how twenty-first century music teaching remains firmly rooted in the musical resources and instructional principles of the 1800s. Printed music, graded learning, isolated technical skills, repertoire study, examinations, teacher direction, drill and repetition, these are all valuable devices that music instructors use in developing students' musicianship. It's also easy to imagine how such instructional principles might produce conflicting outcomes, on the positive side stimulating stable, sequential, and predictable methodologies, while on the negative side promoting student obedience stifled by uniform and impersonal delivery. Yet, many music teachers continue to incorporate these resources and principles because of their proven effectiveness and long track record of success. Tracing these devices to their development in the Scientific and Industrial Revolutions, it's noteworthy that music teaching may benefit from the effectiveness of an assembly line process. And, teachers as supervisors of student development may have practical application. However, such music teaching may have little in common with or relevance to students' genuine musical interests. While there's a noticeable practicality to these resources and principles, it seems they don't really tell the whole story of music teaching. So, how can piano teachers assist students in their musical development without falling into the trap of assembly line teaching practices?

4.2 Piano Teaching and Democratic Relationships

I begin by acknowledging that for certain individuals, democracy may be a concept more associated with notions of government and electoral processes than with musical explorations. Yet, the concept of democracy has significance relevant to music teaching, especially in terms of the values and beliefs teachers may aspire to share with their students in addition to the current trends towards student-centered teaching and project-based learning.

According to music education researcher Allsup, democracy is concerned "with the effort to ensure the equal rights of all members of a given society" (2007, p. 1). Music scholar De Lorenzo describes democracy in terms of the essential freedoms that ensure "human dignity in a good society" (2003, p. 35). In democratic communities, there's an emphasis on cooperation and collaboration rather than competition. People see their stake in others and arrangements are created that encourage people to improve the life of the community by helping others (Apple and Beane 1995, p. 11). Thus, democratic applications reach beyond governmental operations or electoral processes. The ideals of democracy—liberty, equality, and human dignity—are real life attributes that impact the explicit and implicit ways people interact with one another. Each person has the potential to play meaningful roles in fostering, promoting, and protecting democratic ideals in everyday interactions with others.

For music teachers to convey or promote democratic ideals in their teaching, their everyday interactions with students must genuinely comprise liberty, equality, and human dignity. As real life examples of democracy in action, teachers must not only demonstrate the abovementioned characteristics, but also inhabit them honestly and genuinely. They must provide students with an ethical and moral model that encourages independent thinking, appreciation for others, and potential for change. Music teaching helps students prepare for lifelong participation in a democratic society, while imploring and empowering teachers to purposefully embody their own moral and ethical beliefs.

Strong connections between education and democratic teaching may be traced to the iconic 20th century educator Dewey (1859–1952) among others. Known for his advocacy of democracy, Dewey argued for the importance of educational institutions not only as places to gain knowledge, but also to learn how to live.

> The school must itself be a community life in all which that implies. Social perceptions and interests can be developed only in a genuinely social medium—one where there is give and take in the building up of a common experience.... Unless the learning which accrues in the regular course of study affects character, it is futile to conceive the moral end as the unifying and culminating end of education (Dewey 2008, Chap. 26).

Dewey conceived of education as guiding children in acquiring the skills, knowledge, and attitudes to fully participate in a democratic community. Education offers students the qualities that characterize a democratic society: shared interests, freedom in interaction, participation, and social relationships.

Founder of the Suzuki Method of music instruction, Suzuki (1898–1998) advocated the moral dimension associated with democratic relations, envisioning music education as developing "noble hearts and minds in children" and creating "the better world through music" (1969, pp. 7, 114–115). With music study as vehicle for meaningful personal growth, Suzuki emphasized teachers' preparation for guiding students.

> Everything depends on the teacher.... The teacher, if he is a teacher at all, must seriously study... develop himself, correct himself, and make efforts toward his self-growth. In other words, he must be a human presence that ever continues to advance (Suzuki 1982, p. 45).

For Suzuki, democratic teaching relationships are strongly connected to teachers' own intuitive and intentional awareness. Teachers impact their musical community through deliberately critical and reflective self-development.

Education researchers have also indicated that the tone of teacher/student interactions affects how students function in educational environments. An investigation cited by Mueller and Fleming (2001) found that an authoritarian teacher approach resulted in students more academically frustrated, aggressive, and less able to initiate work, whereas democratic teaching relations resulted in students who were happier, more productive and creative (p. 259). In an examination of creativity in elementary music students, Claire (1994) made comparisons between two instructional approaches: hierarchical teaching as incorporating a "linear delineation of power and control over decision making" in contrast to a mutual approach that favors a "collaborative structure for sharing decision making among teachers and students" (p. 23). Claire observed that mutual instructional settings tend to promote voluntary sharing and exploration of ideas in contrast with the control and "getting things right" attitude of hierarchical settings. Thus, democratic teaching relationships may benefit students' cognitive, creative, and social skills while fulfilling the equally significant ideals of equality and human dignity. Democratic instructional relationships begin with teachers' understanding that liberty, equality, and human dignity are living and breathing values that impact how teachers genuinely and thoughtfully inhabit their interactions with students.

Democratic interactions in music instruction are more nuanced than, for example, teachers allowing students to choose between metronome at full speed or half speed, or giving students the opportunity to practise sight reading before technique. Democratic music teachers solicit their students' thoughts and opinions in order to find out what students think, rather than looking for students to regurgitate what teachers think. They invite multiple musical interpretations—ones that endorse students' unconventional explorations and others that reflect our musical traditions.

Unfortunately, many music teachers may be under equipped to implement democratic practices into their teaching because, historically, the authoritarian practice of teaching has occupied a significant portion of music teaching. Teachers become authoritarian in their approach because they equate success as musicians with explicitly following their teachers' authority and controlled outcomes, without acknowledging how such teaching may rob students of the opportunity to critically evaluate or understand their own performances. There's a fear among many music teachers that taking away the discipline associated with teacher authority results in unpredictable, indulgent, and unstable student outcomes, masking as child-centered instruction that caters to the whims of students. What seems possible is that many teachers rely on authoritarian teaching in order to streamline students' learning, in particular to curtail students' acquaintance with things like wrong notes, awkward fingerings, and exaggerated interpretations. It's as if they associate their well-intentioned control of students with security, predictability, and unwavering improvement. Democratic teaching relationships may offer a solution by blending freedom and structure.

In blending freedom and structure, a kind of crosspollination takes place wherein freedom and structure are neither antonyms nor oppositional. They depend on each other to achieve meaningful wholeness, to achieve individual and social significance. As music education philosopher Reimer (2015) explained, it is this interplay between freedom and structure that stimulates and sustains artistic endeavors.

Freedom in the arts is the prerogative, in fact the necessity, for the imagination to range abundantly, widely, and deeply, exploring whatever directions it takes to discover meanings not yet revealed. Yet freedom without structure to give living form to what is being discovered, is empty, an appearance of meaning with no foundation for it to come to life. Structure puts bones into imagination, giving it the wherewithal to survive, to matter, and to be consequential. While freedom without structure is empty, structure without freedom is meaningless…. Our particular obligation as educators is to make available to our students the challenges and delights of musical making and musical sharing, engaging them with the ways of creative thinking and doing that our art depends upon (Reimer 2015, pp. 110–111).

When teachers incorporate freedom and structure, they draw from a blending of their own expertise and their students' interests. They adjust their focus to incorporate traditional musical values while acknowledging such traditions may serve to both stifle and stimulate student's musical experimentation and innovation. As democratic instructors, they pay close attention to their students' likes and dislikes as vital information in order to avoid shutting students out of their learning process. In other words, teachers purposely share their musical expertise with their students, while openly welcoming students' contributions. For example:

> During five-year-old Jordan's first few months of lessons, I focused on meticulously demonstrating piano tone production and technique. In response to my demonstration of fingers scampering on the keyboard, Jordan said, "Looks like spider fingers to me." As his lessons progressed, I welcomed Jordan's descriptive insights ("dinosaur tone, pencil fingers, butterfly tone", and more) many of which I continue to use with other students to this day.
>
> Several years ago, my student Keegan broke down during a lesson performance and exclaimed, "I can't possibly continue when all I'm doing is thinking about all the things I need to get right!" In response, I suggested he consider the dilemma all performers face in "trying to do everything right". How on the one hand, it's a good idea to do things "right", but at the same time, focusing on "doing things right" can result in self-paralysis.
>
> When my student Erica brought up the topic of positive thinking, we discovered that positive thinking has great benefits on the day of performance especially when preceded by critical thinking in the weeks previous. Without some kind of effective preparation, positive thinking could easily lapse into wishful thinking, and we doubted if it could really guarantee successful performance.

What's extraordinary about the above examples is how democratic teachers aren't afraid of students' input, unexpected questioning, and spontaneous developments. These lessons demonstrate how democratic teaching may prompt discussions between students and teachers, how students' thought processes may surface and benefit from teachers' welcoming response. In this approach, music teaching isn't just about getting things "right", it's about guiding students so they may authentically participate in their own development.

Democratic teachers are interested in recognizing and empowering students. They are able to move past the vision of students as necessarily quiet, obedient individuals waiting to be filled with teachers' knowledge. Instead, they recognize that students come with their own ideas about music performance, their own active interests, a desire for experimentation, and fleeting concentration. Democratic teaching isn't about repurposing or reformatting real life students as neutral receptive vessels. It's about the moral and ethical ideals of human dignity and how music teaching gives spark to the flame that is the student's sense of self. Democratic teachers aren't concerned with only doing things the teacher's way. They accept and engage students' input knowing that neither democracy nor musicianship may be defined by a single idyllic and unchanging scenario. Musicianship comes with ups and downs, celebrations and frustrations that serve to remind us of how much we value both our traditions and the unheard musical future.

From this examination, we see how the moral and ethical themes of democratic music teaching stand at a distance from the various models of the 1800s. Democratic teaching distinguishes itself from the predictability and control of authoritarian teaching through an emphasis on cooperation and collaboration. Democratic teachers facilitate cycles of freedom and structure in their teaching, knowing that such a blending encompasses a wide spectrum of highly desirable successful and frequently conflicting outcomes.

4.3   Piano Teaching and the Model of Parenting

Music teaching is an activity with uncanny resemblance to what parents do in raising their children—the lengthy process that incorporates parents' mindful and multilayered involvement as caregiver, guide, protector, and resource. Parents pass on their knowledge of life because they want what's best for their children. They foster their child's self esteem by advocating for and validating their child as a person. They're sensitive to their child's needs, viewpoints, innate characteristics, and abilities. Yet, parenting isn't just about parents attending to their child's desires or needs. Parents also draw from their own values and sense of self in raising their children. They help their children prepare for and understand the joyful and challenging complexities of life by tapping into their own extensive background of parental knowledge and wisdom, while never losing sight of their child's own personal temperament, emotional interests, and social wellbeing.

Similar to the way parents' knowledge and values come into play, music teachers also draw from their own sense of musicianship, musical background, and awareness of music traditions. Likewise, music teachers take into consideration their students' needs, viewpoints, innate characteristics, and abilities in order to support and challenge students' ongoing authentic and independent musical development. This means that music teaching isn't something arbitrarily imposed upon or separate from students. Rather, as students move through the various stages of musical development, teachers pay close attention to their students' musical interests, temperament, and abilities; while with equal importance, teachers tap into their own extensive background of musicianship in order to help students prepare for, appreciate, and participate in lifelong relationships with music.

As children grow to adulthood, the long-term interaction between parents and their children naturally evolves or adjusts in three pertinent ways. Firstly, parents lead the way. Parents begin by leading yet paying attention to where their children might want or need to go. Parents introduce their children to how things may be done—like eating nutritious foods. Secondly, leading turns into handing over, much in response to children's desire to do things for themselves. Parents hand over tasks. They give their children responsibility for getting things done—like feeding themselves. Thirdly, parents expand awareness. They fill in the gaps by expanding their child's awareness, introducing their children to things they might never find on their own—like the subtle flavors of new foods. Using this model of parenting as a guide, music teaching encompasses teachers as leaders of students' musicianship, teachers as handing over the skills of musicianship, and teachers as expanding students' unimagined musicianship. What's fascinating about this music teaching framework—leading, handing over, and expanding—is how each aspect naturally synchronizes with the Stages of Music Learning (Chap. 3).

The Teacher's Role as Leader—When Peter was a student in the Foundation Stage, my principle role was that of leader in terms of tone production, technique, and learning to play by ear—while acknowledging that Peter's active participation was vitally important. Knowing that Peter learned through experimentation, imitation, and meaningful participation, I led through a dual process of demonstrating and recognizing. As demonstrator, I provided Peter with the visual and aural model of what playing the piano looks and sounds like. I showed how to make sound. I demonstrated hand positions and finger movements. I modeled the musical motifs. As Peter's recognizer, I used words and gestures to prompt and validate his role in leading the learning process. I used expressions such as "Show me your..." and "Let me see your..." to reinforce his independence and ownership. I encouraged him in self-evaluation by modeling, by referring to, by asking for, by talking about tone production, how he played, what he played, mistakes, etc. I played along with Peter to strengthen his ability to keep a steady beat. My role of leading paid attention to the practicalities of tone production, technique, and learning by ear without losing track of Peter's personal interests, much like the way parenting draws from parents' values and the child's inherent temperament or personality.

The Teacher's Role in Handing Over—When Peter began the Reading Stage, my role shifted to handing over the skills of musicianship. Specifically, I hand over the skills of tracking the score and keeping the beat at the beginning of the Reading Stage so that students may get comfortable with these skills in relatively easy repertoire. Using this approach, students develop their ownership before encountering repertoire that really requires them to use it. With the musical score as a visual resource, I helped Peter get comfortable with tracking the score with one hand while playing with the other. As Peter's tracking skills progressed week by week, he was soon able to use this skill to work on isolated sections of pieces, making improvements to his fingerings, rhythmic and note accuracy. Handing over also included reinforcing Peter's ability to keep a steady beat by playing with one hand and keeping the beat with the other. Once Peter was accustomed to keeping the most fundamental beat (i.e., four beats in 4/4), I introduced a cyclical process of exploring larger groupings (i.e., two beats per bar and one large beat per bar), always aware that small groupings may be easily handled by small physical movements and large groupings by the entire body. To validate Peter's growing ownership, I continued to use expressions such as "Show me..." and "Let me see your...", with a specific emphasis on statements like "Show me your tracking" and "Let me see you keep the beat" to reinforce his confidence with taking charge of notes, fingerings, beat, expression, and dynamics, in addition to carrying forward his confidence with tone and technique. So, Peter started to do many things for himself that I could do for him, but he might rather I didn't. For example, did Peter really need my assistance to figure out wrong notes, rhythms, or fingerings? If he did, that's all right—because I am definitely there to help him out. But if he didn't, I suspect there's nothing more disempowering than Peter being told he's making mistakes he already knows about.

The Teacher's Role in Expanding—In the expanding stage of formal music instruction, my role was all about furthering Peter's musical awareness. Expanding meant shedding light on areas of musicianship Peter may not access on his own, or had forgotten about, or ways in which Peter might never even consider. Whereas my earlier instruction involved expressions like "Show me..." or "Let me see...", my language in the expanding stage involved a lot of "Tell me about your..." and "What are your thoughts on...". Frequently, I asked Peter, "What should I know about..." or "Can you tell me about..." I used these expressions to find out what Peter practised, how he practised, how successful or unsuccessful he thought about his efforts. In this way, I encouraged Peter to utilize the knowledge and experience he had accumulated throughout his studies. I empowered him to look at how he played, to hear what he played, and talk about his experiences as an emergent musician.

What's remarkable about parent/child interaction as an instructional model is that leading, handing over, and expanding may effectively overlap with each other.

However, an exclusive long-term focus on any one theme may have detrimental effects. For example, leading may be a good thing; and it may also result in students being deprived of the opportunity to develop their own thinking capacity, their own independence, to recognize and validate their own musicianship. Handing over too much information without considering students' readiness may be detrimental to their growth. Similarly, incorporating an expanding perspective too early may inadvertently burden students with expressive requests beyond the scope of students' musical vocabulary and performance skills. That's why leading, handing over, and expanding are always in relation to where students are coming from, what they're doing right now, and where they're heading to in the future.

4.4 Final Thoughts

My goal in this chapter has been to shed light on what music teaching looks like by considering democracy and parenting as models for instruction. This examination suggests that what teachers bring in terms of musical knowledge and expertise is on par with their attitudes, values, and awareness. Teaching draws from the composite of what teachers know, how they interact with others, and who they are.

Looking at the model of democracy, we see the teacher's role has inherently moral and ethical undertones because teachers' attitudes towards others, their values, and awareness of others are embedded in everything they do. The teacher's moral and ethical disposition takes a centrally influential position in teaching. Moreover, teachers don't really have a choice in the matter because even teachers who refuse to take a moral stance or remain neutral on a particular issue send signals to others. When music teachers participate in teaching, they implicitly and explicitly demonstrate their outlook as a combination of aesthetic, moral, intellectual, and reflective dimensions. What comes with a democratic instructional vision is that teachers inhabit teaching as the immense privilege and honor of cultivating humane relations with others, of standing up for their right to dignity, and developing every person's intellectual, spiritual, moral, and aesthetic potential as richly as circumstances and opportunities might allow.

One thing that's remarkable about the parenting model is how parents are always there for their children, through the most ordinary of events, the mundane chores, the hectic routines of everyday life and more. They do what they can to get things done for their children, knowing they must somehow help, support, and challenge children to get things done for themselves. Similarly, music teachers develop meaningful relationships with their students as the foundation for getting things done—from the mundane to the sublime. They pass on their expertise, empowering and equipping their students to do things on their own, to make meaning from their own musical experiences, and continue the musical journey that is already underway.

4.5   Before We Move on

1. Music teaching in the twenty-first century is naturally embedded in our historical past. In what ways does your musical development demonstrate influences related to the advent of printed music and the introduction of compulsory public schooling? How have these movements stimulated and limited your musical development?
2. This chapter examined the democratic principles of liberty, equality, and dignity. In what ways have each of these principles contributed to or been absent from your own musical autobiography? What does this mean for your musical development? Why are these principles important to music teaching?
3. What are some personal examples of *leading, handing over*, and *expanding* from your own musical development? Which one of these approaches do you think currently dominates your teaching? Why?

References

Allsup, R. (2007). Democracy and one hundred years of music education. *Music Educators Journal*, May, 52–56.

Apple, M., & Beane, J. (1995). *Democratic schools*. Alexandria, VA: Association for Supervision and Curriculum Development.

Claire, L. (1994). The social psychology of creativity. *Bulletin of the Council for Research in Music Education, 119,* 21–28.

Davis, B. (2004). *Inventions of teaching*. New York, NY: Laurence Erbaum Associates.

De Lorenzo, L. C. (2003). Teaching music as democratic practice. *Music Educators Journal, 90*(2), 35–40.

Dewey, J. (2008). *Democracy and education*.

Gellrich, M., & Sundin, B. (1993). Instrumental practice in the 18th and 19th centuries. *Council for Research in Music Education, 119,* 137–145.

McPherson, G. E., & Gabrielsson, A. (2002). From sound to sign. In R. Parncutt & G. McPherson (Eds.), *The science and psychology of music performance*. Oxford, UK: Oxford University Press.

Mueller, A., & Fleming, T. (2001). Cooperative learning: Listening to how children work at school. *Journal of Educational Research, 94,* 259–265.

Parakilas, J. (1999). *Three hundred years of life with the piano*. Yale, CT: Yale University Press.

Reimer, B. (2015). Response to Randall Allsup: "Music teacher quality and expertise". *Philosophy of Music Education Review, 23*(1), 108–112.

Suzuki, S. (1982). *Where love is deep*. St. Louis, MS: Talent Education Journal.

Uszler, M., Gordon, S., & Mach, E. (1991). *The well-tempered keyboard teacher*. New York, NY: Schirmer Books.

Chapter 5
Piano Tone and Technique

Abstract Piano tone and technique comprise two inseparable aspects of teachers' work with beginner piano students. Historically, tone has been considered as a most essential ingredient in the world of music because mastery of tone production enables artistic expression. This chapter examines how tone may be characterized as sound vibrations—intensities of energy—that range from soft to loud, light to heavy, bright to dark, short to long, flat to round, and more. Pianists bring immense variations in tonal intensity to their performances by tapping into their emotional, spiritual, intellectual, intuitive, and physical energies. In a departure from treating piano technique as a kind of mechanical training, this chapter considers piano technique as something we may already know about because of how we use our fingers, hands, arms, and body in ordinary everyday life. Specific examples of how beginner piano students may explore five technical basics include: grabbing fingers, walking fingers, arm circles, our body, and appropriate posture at the piano.

5.1 Piano Tone

Although the piano is a percussion instrument, pianists typically talk about the piano's sound as if it were a non-percussive instrument. Often, they refer to the piano's sound by using active words borrowed from the human voice and descriptive terms from the visual, emotional, and tactile world. For example, Hungarian pianist Sandor (1981), who studied with Bartok and Kodaly, described the piano's "ability to talk, to sing, and to shout if necessary, as well as to whisper" (p. 179). Visual descriptors refer to tone in terms of such shapes as flat or round tone, or such colored references as dark, bright, and dull. Emotional descriptors include a vast array of feelings: love, passion, happiness, joy, and sadness. Tactile descriptors include warm, harsh, smooth, heavy, velvety, light. The importance of these descriptors is that they provide a meaningful language for talking about tonal experiences.

Historically, tone has been considered as a most essential ingredient in the world of music because mastery of tone production enables artistic expression. Neuhaus,

M.B. Thompson, *Fundamentals of Piano Pedagogy*,
SpringerBriefs in Education, DOI 10.1007/978-3-319-65533-8_5

renowned teacher at the Moscow Conservatoire, identified tone production as the first and most important among other means of which a pianist should be possessed, while cautioning that tonal mastery remains a means of musical expression, not its purpose. Neuhaus considered tone at the core of music making, entreating musicians to elevate their performances and the inherent value of music by "ennobling and perfecting" tone (1973, p. 56).

The experience of tone may be captured in a simple expression—*intensity of energy*—the idea that tone is characterized by sound vibrations that range in spectrums of *intensity* from soft to loud, light to heavy, bright to dark, short to long, flat to round, playful to serious, jubilant to melancholy, shallow to deep, and more. Tone isn't something we merely hear as commonplace sound. We perceive or interpret tone in terms of intensities that have aesthetic and personal significance. For example, we experience the intensity of tone as having qualities from beautiful to ugly, pleasing to displeasing, sympathetic to harsh. So when music teachers make reference to a round, sonorous sound, we know that such depictions call for a particular intensity of tonal energy in performing and listening. When music teachers ask that the sound should carry, or have a body, or be expressive, or ring, or have a lasting quality, they're talking about the way performers can directly influence tonal intensities by transforming their own personal energy into sound.

What seems extraordinary in approaching tone as intensity of energy is that pianists bring immense variations in intensity to their performances by tapping into their emotional, spiritual, intellectual, intuitive, and physical energies. They play from the heart, mind, and soul of who they are. Tone and technique embody the energy of sound and the performer's individual energy. Yet, pianists rely on their fingers, hands, forearm, whole arm, and whole body as the practical physical means for generating tone. They transform the multilayered physicality of piano performance into the vibrating energy of sound. That explains why music teachers spend so much time focusing on tone and technique—because tone and technique are intimately bound to each other through intensities of energy.

5.2 Piano Technique

Ever since Bartolommeo Cristofori constructed the *Gravicemabalo col piano e forte* in 1709, there has been ample ongoing discussion amongst performers and teachers regarding piano technique. Clementi (1752–1832), Czerny (1791–1857), Matthay (1858–1945), Breithaupt (1873–1956), Cortot (1877–1962), Neuhaus (1888–1964), Ortmann (1889–1979), Gieseking (1895–1956), Kochevitschy (1903–93), Sandor (1912–2005), Gát (1913–67), Bernstein (b. 1927), and Fink (b. 1929) are just a few of the iconic musicians who have contributed to our understanding of the diverse physical aspects involved in piano technique. Some aspects are concerned with finger articulation, while others promote arm weight and relaxation, while still others involve a multilayering of physiological mechanics.

Certain approaches incorporate scientific research, while others draw from highly personalized idiosyncratic pedagogical approaches.[1]

My goal is to examine piano technique as something we may already know about because of how we use our fingers, hands, arms, and body in ordinary everyday life. This means that piano technique is something familiar and normal based on the fundamental actions, movements, and motions of our body. This approach stands in direct contrast to the literature's tendency for treating piano technique in terms of specifically acquired actions or piano technique as a kind of mechanical training in keeping with the piano's mechanical construction. However, in exploring how ordinary everyday motions can contribute to piano technique, I want to stress that piano technique is not merely a matter of physical movements. As discussed above, intellectual, spiritual, emotional, and intuitive energies are involved as well. Furthermore, I want to emphasize that piano technique isn't an end in itself; rather, it's a very important and relevant tool in tone production, making music, and expressing ourselves as musicians. As *From the Stage to the Studio* (2012) music lecturer Cornelia Watkins and professor of music Laurie Scott have affirmed, all technique exists to serve the music and all musicians must listen. Aural feedback is what tells us whether our technique is doing what it is supposed to do (p. 41). The whole point of developing piano technique is so that we may bring to life our relevant thoughts, motives, and feelings in personally meaningful and rewarding musical expressions. In the following sections, I describe five basics from ordinary everyday life that I introduce to all my beginner students during their first year of piano lessons.

5.2.1 Basic #1: Grab and Release

Most of the time in ordinary everyday life, we don't really think about what we're physically doing with our hands or our fingers. Most likely, we're concerned with what we want to accomplish by using our hands, things like locking the door, washing our face, putting on our shoes, brushing our teeth, and the list goes on and on. To say that we use our hands or our fingers a lot is something of an understatement. In ordinary everyday life, we use our hands and fingers all the time and in an infinite number of ways. Grasp, grab, hold, let go, pick up, hug, stroke, grip, drop, caress, rub, press, touch, pinch, flick, pat, tap, and poke. Each of these motions is a descriptive variation of the universal capacity we all have to grab and release. Just take a look at an infant the next time you have the opportunity and you might observe something remarkable yet easily overlooked: the child's fingers ever so gently grabbing and releasing. It's almost as if the child's purposeful preparation for a lifetime of using his or her hand is already underway.

---

[1]On the topic of piano tone and technique, see: Bernstein (1981, 1991), Breithaupt (1909), Clementi (1973), Cortot (1928), Czerny (1839), Fink (1992), Gieseking and Leimer (1972), Kochevitshy (1967), and Matthay (1903).

When it comes to piano technique, the question is—How do these basic motions of grabbing and releasing transfer to the piano? Start by examining your own hand's grabbing and releasing motions. You'll notice that when you grab, your fingers and thumb converge in the palm of your hand from different directions. Your fingers grab from the top of the palm while your thumb grabs from the palm's side. The grabbing motion requires a certain amount of engagement dependent upon how much and how long you grab. Release occurs by letting go of the fingers and thumb, or by lengthening the fingers and thumb in order to open the hand.

At the piano, the performer's ability to grab and release has immediate application. For the fingers, because the length of the key is parallel to the fingers, it's easy for fingers to grab the key (depress the key) to produce a sound, and release the key (let the key come back up) to terminate a sound. For the thumb, grabbing and releasing involves moving the thumb across the key's width rather than its length. This is in keeping with what you noticed above—that fingers and thumb create the grabbing function by converging in the palm from different directions. What's remarkable about producing sound in this way is that every person has ample experience in grabbing and releasing motions long before they ever get to the piano. They also understand the subtle but important differences between grabbing a feather, an ice cream cone, and a dog's tail; and likewise the differences between releasing a pencil, a balloon, and a glass of water. Using grabbing and releasing motions for piano technique and producing sound at the piano is a continuation of how we basically use our hands and fingers in ordinary everyday life.

One of the discussions that frequently appears in literature on piano technique has to do with using curved or straight fingers (Gát 1965; Ortmann 1925; Parncutt and Troup 2002). By paying attention to fingers that grab/release, I've noticed that using curved or straight fingers takes on a new meaning—that piano technique isn't so much a matter of how we *hold* our fingers in one position or another. Rather, piano technique involves fingers that are constantly *moving* to create tonal intensities by adjusting the velocity, the fullness, and the subtlety of grabbing and releasing. As Ortmann described, piano playing is all about "movement, not position" (1925, p. 33). At any moment, you might be able to take a picture of curved or straight fingers, but in the overall process of tone production, the terms grabbing and releasing provide the most accurate description of the movements our fingers go through. Additionally, grabbing and releasing is always in relation to the intensity of tone we desire in performance as in the following scenario:

At Natalie's first lesson, I helped her to explore grabbing fingers with an introductory non-legato tonalization (detached sound). However, when Natalie demonstrated her non-legato tonalization during her second lesson, I realized her enthusiasm for grabbing fingers completely overshadowed her listening. In place of the calm tone and gently grabbing fingers of week one, Natalie played with an abrupt sound and flicking fingers. "Let's listen to see which one has calm tone and which one has flicking tone", I said before demonstrating the two variations in sound. "Both have grabbing fingers", I added just to make sure Natalie got my point. It was a good reminder for me that developing fluency with grabbing fingers always needed to consider the desired tone quality.

A few months later, Natalie's fluency in grabbing fingers would be essential in playing solid triads with the left hand. Initially, Natalie stiffened her fingers, pushing them into the keys in order to play a solid chord. "Let's try just two fingers, 1 and 3, with grabbing," I suggested. "They can hug the keys and we'll listen to the gentle tone." And so, we tried different combinations: 1 and 3, 1 and 5, 3 and 5, before attempting 1, 3, and 5 all together. Always listening for the tone quality.

5.2.2 Basic #2: Walking Fingers

Although I use the term "walking fingers", this particular technical aspect is concerned with the arm's role in tone and technique. In a manner similar to the above examination, it seems we may not really think about what we physically do with our arms in ordinary everyday life. Instead, we might be more concerned with what we want to accomplish by using our arms, like reaching for a book on a shelf, opening and closing a door, reaching out to shake hands, moving the iron back and forth as we iron our clothes, and more. In these examples, our arms function in terms of lengthening and shortening or reaching out and retracting motions. Our arms move in, out, down, up, to the back, to the front, on one side, the other side, farther, and closer. Through a lengthening and shortening or reaching out and retracting motions we move, position, place, and reposition our hands/fingers in many directions and locations.

So, in terms of piano technique, the question is—How does this basic aspect of lengthening/shortening transfer to the piano? Let's begin with an experiment related to the arm's function of lengthening and shortening that involves a simple comparison.

1. Sit in a comfortable position with your hands resting on your mid-thigh. Let your hand take a spider shape (your fingers are the spider legs, the back of your hand is the spider body). Let your hands/fingers comfortably grab and release in *walking forward and backward* with your spider fingers on your thigh. Let your forearm follow along. Be conscious of the energy in your hands and fingers.
2. Sit in a comfortable position with your hands resting on your mid-thigh. Once again, let your hand take a spider shape. This time, let your hands/fingers comfortably grab and release as you *walk in place* with your spider fingers on your thigh. Do not go forward or backward, only grab and release with your fingers and thumbs. Be conscious of the energy in your hands and fingers.

For over 30 years, I've been asking teachers and students to perform this experiment always with the same results. Specifically, that it's easier for your hands/fingers to grab/release when your arm is in motion. It's easier to play the piano with *walking* hands/fingers than with hands/fingers held in position by stationary arms.

In *The Craft of Piano Playing* (2002), Alan Fraser describes a similar experiment using wiggling fingers with the same conclusion. He explains "putting your arm in motion frees all its muscles to activate more effectively, even those involved not in the arm movement itself but in finger movement" (p. 144). In other words, it's physically easier to move your fingers when the arm's muscles are actively in motion than when the arm's muscles are held in place. This exploration has important implications for piano technique in two overlapping ways: (1) in terms of how we use our hands/fingers, and (2) in terms of how we consider hand position as a stationary matter or as a moving matter.

Firstly, in terms of how we use our hands/fingers. Acknowledging that it's easier to grab/release with our fingers when we lengthen and shorten our arms, I use the expression *walking* fingers to facilitate this exploration with my students. That means we explore the keyboard by using walking fingers to travel from any place on the key to the fallboard, and back again, and forward again, and more as beneficial. We use walking fingers to move in big steps and small steps as appropriate, taking care and having fun to exaggerate how much and how little we can walk with our fingers. Walking fingers is equally versatile in its application to one finger playing repeated notes or to combinations of fingers playing. The point is that lengthening and shortening our arms or walking fingers allows for greater freedom and agility in grabbing/releasing our hands/fingers.

Secondly, in terms of how we consider hand position as a stationary matter or as a moving matter. Here, I appreciate Ortmann's reminder that piano technique isn't so much a matter of position or how we *hold* our hands/fingers, as it is about how we *move* our arms and hands/fingers in ways that promote freedom and agility. Looking at the natural connection between lengthening/shortening our arms and facility in using our hands/fingers, we see the immediate deficiencies in thinking of hand position as a stationary placement. This is because in holding our hands/fingers in place, we greatly limit or restrict their potential freedom and agility. It's a limitation that Thomas Mark identified repeatedly as a danger in *What Every Pianist Needs to Know about the Body* (2003). Thinking of hand position as a moving matter prompts an interesting shift in our awareness—one that considers hand position as the motions we use to travel the length of the 6-inch white key and the 4-inch black key. From this perspective, hand position refers to the stable way I move my hand/fingers rather than the insistence on a specific shaping of the hand. While walking fingers might seem counterproductive to a stable or supportive hand position, my experience indicates that using walking fingers is enormously beneficial in taking advantage of the arm's practical connection to the hand/fingers. We gain stability in hand position not by confining the hand's movements, but by including the arm as a natural and welcome participant in piano technique. By combining the action of lengthening/shortening our arms and the motion of walking fingers, we develop piano technique that allows for maximal finger agility and freedom while paying attention to the need for a stable yet completely moveable hand position.

I introduced seven-year-old Spencer to walking fingers around his third or fourth lesson. Initially, I showed him walking with fingers 2 and 3 stepping from the edge of the key to the fallboard and back, prior to exploring fingers 3 and 4, 4 and 5, and finally thumb and finger 2. During his weekly lessons, I'd check his walking fingers and encourage him to continue walking in his home practice.

Approximately one month later and after Spencer had completed several right hand legato melodies, I noticed his wrist consistently dropped below the keyboard soon after he launched into a melody. I asked him to try walking fingers in the first few bars of each piece. Remarkably, as long as Spencer used walking fingers, his wrist never dropped below the keyboard. Of course, sometimes Spencer's fingers got caught up in the black keys, but with each passing week, the black keys and dropping his wrist became less of an issue. His moving arm provided the necessary wrist support. My responsibility was to come up with creative ways to revisit walking fingers as an ongoing and valuable technical exploration.

One year later, when Spencer encountered scales in his repertoire, I once again noticed his wrist dropping whenever he played with his thumb. I pointed out how walking forward with his thumb could provide a solution. It was a small adjustment with an immediately positive impact on his playing. Thus, walking fingers became and has remained an important part of Spencer's ongoing technical development.

5.2.3   Basic #3: Arm Circles

Continuing the exploration of how we use our arms, another perspective comes into play. This time I want to consider how we use our arms in horizontal actions like stirring a pot of soup, wiping a counter top, and more. Try these exercises for yourself:

1. Sit in a comfortable position at the piano. Move your forearms horizontally in a circular motion over the keyboard. Pay attention to the energy in your hand/fingers and arms.
2. Sit in a comfortable position at the piano. Move your forearms horizontally in a straight line parallel to the keyboard. Pay attention to the energy in your hand/fingers and arms.

What difference do you feel between moving in a circular motion and moving in a straight line? Which motion feels easier? Why do circular motions feel less intrusive and more comfortable than straight line motions? The answer to this final question is remarkable. Circular motions feel more comfortable because they move only in one direction (round and round), because they have no end, and because there is no stopping involved in circular motions. In contrast, straight line motions actually move in two directions (one going and one coming). Straight line motions incorporate a readjustment in encountering two end points and straight lines motions naturally consist of multiple movements in terms of moving, stopping, and reversing. So, once again in terms of piano technique, the question is—How does this basic aspect of circular arm motion transfer to the piano?

What I appreciate about the above comparison between circular and straight line arm motions is that it builds on the previous exploration of walking fingers. Recognizing the difference between circular and straight line motion is important because it sheds light on the difference between piano technique based on the body's natural motions and piano technique based on the construction of the piano. Of course, when we look at the piano, we see the keys arranged in nothing but straight lines. So, it might seem logical that our corresponding motions at the piano would also be based on straight lines. Yet, in exploring the difference between straight line and circular motions, it's easy to see how using circular motions reinforces piano technique in keeping with the body's natural movements. As Neuhaus (1973) explained, "The shortest path between two points on the keyboard is a curve" (p. 132). Neuhaus' statement might be interpreted as—the most *natural movement* between two points on the keyboard is a curve.

> I introduced six-year-old Aleesha to circles in an elementary piece with a left hand broken octave ostinato pattern of Low C—Bass C—Low C—Bass C. Played by finger 5 (Low C) and thumb (Bass C), I showed her how to use a counterclockwise circular arm motion wherein finger 5 moved/grabbed from the fallboard to the key edge and thumb moved/grabbed from the key edge to the fallboard in a continuous cycle. (In contrast, right hand arm circles incorporate a clockwise circular motion.) This circular arm motion was beneficial given the smallness of Aleesha's left hand, in particular as it avoided the tension caused by stretching her hand beyond its natural limitations.

5.2.4   Basic #4: Our Body

Looking at piano technique as more than fingers/hands/arms, the aspect of how we use our body comes into play. Here, I'm thinking about how we use our body in swinging a bat, throwing an object, bouncing a ball, and more. When we use our body, we are able to draw additional strength and weight from the larger muscles of our arms and shoulders and the weight of our body mass. We use our body to facilitate an entire array of pulling, pushing, lifting, hitting, bouncing, pressing, free falling, thrusting, and diving movements. We draw energy from breathing in and out. And, we may also tap into the immense store of energy in our own internal core—our own emotional, spiritual, intuitive, and physical grounding. I incorporate this aspect into my own teaching in order to expand my students' palette of sound qualities.

Using our body to increase energy, strength, weight, and mass makes up an important part of piano technique in terms of two highly valued physical motions—down and up.

To explore *downward* motion with my student Garrett towards the middle of his first year of piano lessons, I used the example of a belly flop where a person stands at the edge of a diving board and simply falls into the water. My demonstration included: (1) raising my hand above the keyboard, (2) getting ready to drop, and (3) belly flopping with my hand/fingers into the keyboard. Then, I demonstrated a piano belly flop with only one finger depressing a key as my hand fell into the keyboard. I demonstrated a piano belly flop with my finger grabbing the key as it depressed the key, therein making sure to cushion the pressure of my arm. Finally, I demonstrated what happens when I add my entire body to the belly flop process. After each demonstration, I asked Garrett to try out his own piano belly flop and together we enjoyed the excitement of sharing a new exploration. "Did you notice how the tone has changed," I'd ask. We would compare belly flop tone to our usual tone, compare the difference between belly flopping without a grabbing finger and belly flopping with a grabbing finger, and make note of a belly flop with the arm and a belly flop with our entire body.

To explore *upward* motion with Garrett, I used the experience of jumping on a trampoline and the burst of energy that propels the body upward to inspire our explorations. I demonstrated the trampoline exercise by (1) placing my hand on my lap (the trampoline), and (2) using a burst of arm/body energy to propel my arm upward. Similarly, after placing my hand on the keyboard (the trampoline), I used a combination of grabbing finger and arm/body energy to propel my arm upward. "Give it a try," I'd say to Garrett and we'd talk about the tone, in particular comparing the sound when there's no arm/body energy involved and when there's lots of arm/body energy involved. We made note of the difference between a trampoline that involves only the arm and a trampoline that explodes from our internal core.

In exploring these basic downward and upward motions, it's vitally important for me to pay attention to the core of my body—the physically grounded place in the lower third of my torso—because as Ortmann's research revealed, the smallest movement of piano technique involves the "trunk as well as the arm, hand, and fingers" (1925, p. 71). Made up of diverse muscle groups, the nervous system, and numerous bones, the core occupies the area above the pelvis and the base of the spine. Involving the core of my body is essential in downward and upward motions, especially in terms of stabilizing and mobilizing piano performance. In downward motions, I consider the core as the anchor for my entire body. It's the physical grounding that holds me in place, providing stability and a kind of centered energy. I use the anchoring energy in my core to bring additional strength, weight and mass to my hands/fingers as appropriate to an entire palette of tone colors. While from the upward motion perspective, the core of my body acts as a kind of energy mobilizer for tone production. Here, I use my core as the support in lifting, propelling, and carrying the movements of my torso, arms, and hands/fingers.

Using my core as an anchor and mobilizer, I bring attention to breathing in and out. Watch what happens to your core when you inhale and exhale. When you take breath into your lungs, there's an immediate feeling of upwardness, a lifting of your torso as supported by your core. When you exhale, it's interesting to observe how your torso sinks into the core, resulting in a kind of fortification of the core or grounding of your anchor. When you change the speed of inhaling and exhaling, there's a corresponding modification to the intensity of sound and the intentionality of piano performance on many different levels. As pianist Arrau described, "phrasings have to do with the movement of breathing" (1982, p. 102). Similarly, Sandor affirmed, "The closest connecting link between the performing apparatus and music itself is breathing, which guides and controls both the phrasing and the pace of muscular activities" (1981, pp. 30–31). How we use our core/breath is intimately and indisputably connected to our thought processes, our emotional heartfelt feelings, our physical experiences, our sense of spirituality, and more.[2] For example, on an emotional level, just watch how emotions may transform the engagement of your core/breath into purposeful and meaningful movements, as well as infinite tonal colors. On another level, watch what happens when you introduce a spiritual or soulful meaning to the gestures of core/breath. Appreciate how the intensity of sound and the intentionality of your performance may be influenced by the way your core/breath takes up a spiritual direction.

Examining the movements of down and up, the core as stabilizer and mobilizer, breathing in and out, the dynamics of thought, emotion, and spirituality—certain things stand out. Firstly, I like the idea of how down and up are inseparable from each other; how inhaling and exhaling follow each other; how the core as stabilizer permits mobility, and mobility depends on stability; how thoughts, emotions, physicality, and spirituality overlap with each other, sometimes with tension and at other times in synchronization. These basic aspects benefit from reciprocal connections that take advantage of the ebb and flow of relationships rather than the dominance of a one-rule approach. Secondly, what stands out for me is the familiarity we have with each one of these aspects of piano technique—downward and upward movements, our core as anchor and mobilizer, breathing in and out, our

---

[2]For further examination of the interrelation between breathing, movement, and musical expression, see Pierce and Pierce (1989, pp. 167–194).

emotions and spirituality. While these aspects of ordinary everyday life play important roles in piano technique, they also demonstrate who we are as persons, the way we express ourselves, the attitude and outlook we carry through life. Just think about how every person moves, or breathes, or takes on emotional situations. These aspects are shared by all of us, yet, we acknowledge that each person has his or her own signature ways of moving, breathing, and responding to emotional situations. So, I want to develop piano technique in a way that's familiar by using these aspects from ordinary everyday life. Using this approach, piano technique isn't something foreign that we take on as an artificial requirement. Piano technique involves tapping into universal ways of moving, breathing, and emotional responses while welcoming each person's individually authentic and genuine desire for expressing who they are as a person.

5.2.5   Basic #5: Posture

As an aspect of piano technique, the performer's piano posture plays an undeniably important role (Bastien 1973, pp. 124–5). Piano posture can either enable or restrict the performer's ability to control or manipulate tone production in an efficient and personally expressive way. A comprehensive approach to posture takes into consideration the performer's entire body from head to toe, even though the performer's hands/fingers, arms, and torso are the most practically involved. While literature on the topic of piano posture is vast, there is general agreement on several guiding principles: (1) the body sits comfortably upright and balanced, (2) the forearm is parallel to the floor, (3) height of the forearm is in line with the keyboard, and (4) feet are grounded on the floor. These principles are not to be interpreted in a fixed or immovable manner, rather, as a basic setup that allows for the ebb and flow of appropriate movements. Pianist Gyorgy Sandor provided the following guidance:

> In maintaining our balance at the piano we seek both stability and mobility; we also seek minimum effort in maintaining balance at the piano. By *stability* I mean a position that enables us to sit comfortably, and by *mobility* I mean a position that enables us to move freely and effortlessly all over the keyboard. Most of the body weight rests on the bench, but some of it is support by the feet, especially when the body is in motion. Whenever our hands are in motion, the balance of the body changes, even though the change is very slight (1981, p. 31).

Taking into consideration this concise view of piano posture, I draw attention to a pertinent drawback related to the dimensions of the piano—specifically, an issue in terms of the height of the keyboard and the height of the bench. The drawback being that the piano and its bench have been designed for adults, rather than designed for children. Generally speaking, the dimensions of pianos and benches are consistent with the keyboard of a piano at 28 inches from the floor and the bench height at 19 inches from the floor. While these dimensions may be appropriate for most adult performers, the physical proportioning of most children under the age of 13 means they'll require a minimal bench height of 21 inches in order to position the forearm parallel to the floor and in line with the keyboard.

Try the following exercises for yourself:

1. At the piano, perform any musical selection while seated on a bench that has been lowered two or more inches from your usual height. Take notice of alterations in your piano technique.
2. Sit on a table or counter top that can support weight. Let your feet dangle as you sit with your arms in piano performance position. Take notice of how you feel, particularly in your thighs and lower back.

In *What Every Pianist Needs to Know about the Body*, Thomas Mark explained how a person sitting too low may "hunch the shoulders or lift the elbows or clench the fingers as if to grab the piano" (p. 53). Unfortunately, such actions compromise the ability to use our arms, hands, and fingers in the natural ways we have explored thus far. Similarly, when children sit with dangling feet, the effort of sitting balanced upright puts pressure on their thighs. That's why many children tend to slouch when sitting with feet dangling, because slouching relieves or reduces pressure on the thighs.

Fortunately, any mismatch in seating can easily be resolved by using an adjustable piano chair with a height of 21 inches or more and by supporting the child's feet with a footstool at an appropriate height. It's a suggestion that Czerny put forward nearly two centuries ago in his *Letters to Young Ladies on the Art of Playing the Piano Forte* (1837). "And if your feet should not reach the ground, have a dwarf stool, or ottoman, made of a proper height, to place them on" (p. 5).

5.3 Final Thoughts

This chapter has focused on piano technique through the familiar and natural ways we use our fingers, hands, arms, and body in ordinary everyday life. This approach has an immediate and ongoing practicality for beginner piano students, as pianist Camp (1981) described, "piano teaching should involve the presentation of concepts which will appear over and over again in more complex settings throughout a student's musical experience." (p. 2). Consequently, I repeatedly engage my students in increasingly sophisticated explorations of piano tone and technique from their first efforts as beginners to their thoughtful interpretations as advanced performers. Grabbing fingers is an application that I've found to be beneficial in everything from a simple legato melody, to the solid chords in Schumann's *The Happy Farmer* opus 68 #10, and the staccato accompaniment of Kabalevsky's *Song of the Cavalry* opus 27 #29. Walking fingers may assist with wrist stability in repertoire from *Mary had a Little Lamb* to the 16th note scale passages in Mozart's *K.331 Rondo alla Turca*. Using arm circles means I'm able to provide students with a practical alternative to over-stretching their hands, no matter how manageable or unmanageable the leaps. Furthermore, downward and upward movements, the core as anchor and mobilizer, breathing in and out, emotions and spirituality are aspects of daily life that have practical application for beginners and beyond. In this way, the process of teaching piano technique involves a long trajectory of revisiting the fundamental ways we use our body—all with the goal of producing the intensities of resonant energy I refer to as tone.

5.4 Before We Move on

1. Tone production has been considered a most essential ingredient in the world of music because it enables artistic expression. How has your musical development been shaped by the exploration of tone production?
2. How does the expression of tone as *intensity of energy* align your own interpretation of tone?
3. Piano technique involves the familiar and natural ways we use our fingers, hands, arms, and body in ordinary everyday life. How do you feel about this theme of everyday movements? For non-keyboard musicians, how does this focus on everyday motions shed light on your technical approach to tone production?
4. This chapter examined using the core as an anchor and mobilizer with particular attention to breathing in and out. How is this aspect evident in your own experience as a musician?

References

Arrau, C. (1982). *Conversations with Arrau.* New York, NY: Alfred A. Knopf.

Bastien, J. W. (1973). *How to teach piano successfully.* Park Ridge, IL: Kjos.

Bernstein, S. (1981). *With your own two hands.* New York, NY: Schirmer.

Bernstein, S. (1991). *Twenty lessons in keyboard choreography.* Milwaukee, IL: Hal Leonard.

Breithaupt, R. (1909). *Natural piano technic* (Trans. J. Bernhoff). Leipzig: Kahnt Nachfolger.

Camp, M. (1981). *Developing piano performance: A teaching philosophy.* Chapel Hill, NC: Hinshaw Music.

Clementi, M. (1973). *Introduction to the art of playing the pianoforte.* New York, NY: Da Capo Press.

Cortot, A. (1928). *Rational principles of pianoforte technique* (Trans. Le Roy-Metaxas). Paris, FR: Salabert.

Czerny, C. (1837). *Letters to young ladies on the art of playing the piano forte.* Boston, MA: Oliver Ditson.

Czerny, C. (1839). *Complete theoretical and practical piano forte school.* London, UK: R. Cocks.

Fink, S. (1992). *Mastering piano technique: A guide for students, teachers, and performers.* Portland, OR: Amadeus Press.

Fraser, A. (2002). *The craft of piano playing: A new approach to piano technique.* Oxford, UK: The Scarecrow Press.

Gát, J. (1965). *The technique of piano playing*. Budapest: Corvina.

Gieseking, W., & Leimer, K. (1972). *Piano technique*. New York, NY: Dover.

Kochevitsky, G. (1967). *The art of piano playing: A scientific approach*. Evanston, IL: Summy-Birchard.

Mark, T. (2003). *What every pianist needs to know about the body*. Chicago, IL: GIA Publications.

Matthay, T. (1903). *The art of touch*. London, UK: Longmans.

Neuhaus, H. (1973). *The art of piano playing*. Wolfeboro, NH: Longwood Academic.

Ortmann, O. (1925). *The physical basis of piano touch and tone*. New York, NY: E. Dutton.

Parncutt, R., & Troup, M. (2002). Piano. In R. Parncutt & G. McPherson (Eds.), *The science and psychology of music performance*. Oxford, UK: Oxford University Press.

Pierce, A., & Pierce, R. (1989). *Expressive movement: Posture and action in daily life, sports, and the performing arts*. New York, NY: Insight Books.

Sandor, G. (1981). *On piano playing*. New York, NY: Schirmer.

Watkins, C., & Scott, L. (2012). *From the stage to the studio: How fine musicians become great teachers*. Oxford, UK: Oxford University Press.

Chapter 6
Teaching the Student

Abstract An important aspect of teaching beginner piano students may be described in terms of teaching the student as different from teaching the repertoire. This approach specifically involves the teacher's ability to go beyond the repertoire to stimulate comprehensive student musical development. Also relevant to the aspect of teaching the student is the accumulated repertoire approach wherein students review and refine pieces they know how to play, instead of dropping pieces after they've been learned. Teaching the student may also require teachers to consider their roles as student advocators and agitators. Advocating is all about welcoming students into unconditional learning processes that respect students' personality. As agitators, teachers challenge their students by taking them beyond their comfort zone. Finally, this chapter examines what happens when students' concern shifts from fulfilling their own self-interests to care for the wellbeing of music.

Music teaching is a complex and multilayered endeavor that teachers take on for many different reasons. Some teachers feel an empowered connection to musical sounds, tones, and textures. Some teachers love working with children. They experience immense satisfaction in encouraging children of all ages in musical explorations. Other teachers acknowledge their commitment to tradition, operating as respectful stewards who protect, carry, and pass on the legacy of our musical past. For others, it's the repertoire no matter how modest or grand that pulls them to teach. And of course, there are many teachers for whom it's the instrument itself that underscores their passionate embrace, the way it feels in their hands and alters their breath. Teachers bring multiple perspectives to their teaching, some of which have a lot to do with teaching musical repertoire and some of which focus on teaching the student.

My goal in this chapter is to examine what it means to teach the student as something that differs from teaching the repertoire, while acknowledging that for some teachers, it may be difficult and even undesirable to separate teaching students from teaching music content. In recent years, educational researchers have been particularly attentive to this idea in terms of promoting the difference between

M.B. Thompson, *Fundamentals of Piano Pedagogy*,
SpringerBriefs in Education, DOI 10.1007/978-3-319-65533-8_6

curriculum-centered (also know as knowledge-based or content-based) teaching and learner-centered (student-centered) teaching (Caposey 2014; Weimer 2013). In the former example, knowledge is an object/thing and teaching involves delivering content by telling "students what to do, giving orders, and directing practice" (Davis et al. 2015, pp. 45–46). In the latter, teaching is less about transmission of information and more about transformation of students. Students are no longer passive agents to be controlled. Teachers present students with choices, challenges, and tasks appropriate to engage students as active participants in their own learning experiences (Ibid, pp. 107–08).

So, what does this mean for teachers of beginner piano students? How does teaching the student differ from teaching the repertoire? Take a look at the following scenarios and see if you can figure out which teacher is teaching the student and which is teaching musical repertoire.

Scenario One: Student plays through Beethoven *Sonatina in G major: First movement*. Teacher says, "This piece needs more dynamic contrast on the last page. Play that section again, please." Student responds by playing forte and piano in the designated bars. Teacher says, "Could you make your forte sound more like this? In performing Beethoven, your arms should move like this." Teacher demonstrates and student imitates teacher's demonstration. Teacher says, "That's what that section needs. Now try to make your piano softer like this. See how I move my fingers." Teacher demonstrates and student imitates teacher's demonstration. Teacher says, "Nicely done. Now just practice those sections like that ten times daily at home."

Scenario Two: Student plays through Beethoven *Sonatina in G major: First movement*. Teacher says, "Let's explore some dynamics on page 2. I'm curious to see how loud you can play the *forte* section." Student responds by playing *forte* in the designated bars. Teacher says, "Sure. Let's see what happens when we use our arms to play *forte*." Teacher demonstrates and student imitates teacher's demonstration. Teacher says, "Got it. What happens when you use your whole body?" Student experiments. Teacher says, "Cool. What about *piano*? How about just fingertips?" Teacher demonstrates and student imitates teacher's demonstration. Teacher says, "Okay. What about no-tone?" Student experiments. Teacher says, "Nice. Why don't you practice ten times arms, ten times whole body, ten times fingertips, and ten times no-tone every day and see where you get to for next week."

At first glance, it may seem as if there is, in fact, no difference between the above scenarios. In both situations, teacher and student engage in an exploration of dynamics. Both scenarios incorporate affirmative statements and demonstrations. Yet, there is a subtle and significant difference between Scenario One and Two. Namely, that Scenario One explores forte and piano only as they apply to the performance of Beethoven's *Sonatina*, whereas Scenario Two explores forte and piano from a much larger, investigative, and more personal perspective belonging to the student. Scenario Two's teacher deliberately initiates the exploration of *Sonatina* as an opportunity to refine the student's evolving tonal mastery. This teacher uses the music of Beethoven as a launching pad for teaching the student, recognizing that comprehensive student musicianship includes more than *Sonatina's* specific performance needs.

With the goal of looking at teaching the student from several perspectives, this chapter addresses—what separating repertoire needs from student needs might look like, the accumulated repertoire approach to developing students' mastery of musicianship, teachers as advocates and agitators, and how caring for music comes into play as part of teaching students.

6.1 Separating Students' Development from Repertoire Requirements

One of the most vital aspects concerned with teaching beginner students may be described in terms of the teacher's ability to separate teaching the student from teaching the repertoire. This means teachers differentiate between students' development as musicians and performance requirements dictated by the repertoire. For example, teachers who separate teaching the student from teaching the repertoire make the distinction between teaching articulation in Schumann's *Wild Rider* and developing fluent articulation as part of students' entire range of musicianship. They recognize how teaching rhythmic control in Beethoven's *Ode to Joy* is different from developing students' own internal sense of pulse.

When piano teachers purposefully separate students' development from repertoire requirements, they stimulate and reinforce students' fluency with two basic musical aspects: tone quality and rhythmic continuity. In this respect, they follow the example of Heinrich Neuhaus from the Moscow Conservatoire, who asserted:

> Tone and rhythm go hand in hand, help each other and only jointly can they solve the problem of ensuring an expressive performance (1973, p. 53).

Tone quality and rhythmic continuity (also known as the beat or pulse) form the foundation of students' musical development. (For vocal and non-keyboard instrumental instructors, the aspect of intonation is also paramount.)

Even before students begin learning to play a musical instrument, they're already well acquainted with tone and rhythm from their everyday experiences of life. They know how the tone quality of their parents' voices may change the meaning of words and how their own inflections will indicate whether they're asking a question or making a statement. They've experienced rhythmic continuity in walking, running, and dancing, as well as the rhythm of language. They know how the meaning of words may change with the beat of language.

In my own teaching, I build on students' prior rhythmic experiences by engaging my students in the basics of feeling the beat, encouraging them to integrate their internal rhythmic beat with clapping their hands or moving their bodies. In keeping with the influential American piano teacher Whiteside (1881–1956), an all-encompassing rhythm "must be at the bottom of all beautiful music" (1961, p. 4). Similarly, pianist Max Camp proposed, "A student can learn to make music only if a rhythmic impulse is generated in that person and the ear is brought to life" (1981, p. 49). During the Foundation Stage of learning (Chap. 3) and the leading stage of teaching (Chap. 4), I play the repertoire along with my students, providing them with a kind of stable rhythmic anchor. With students in the Reading Stage of learning, I start handing over the ability to play with one hand and keep the beat with the other, while never forgetting the advantage of playing along with students, or getting off the piano bench to dance, swing, or march through a piece. By returning again and again to explorations of the beat, I deliberately and progressively reinforce students' rhythmic awareness and control in increasingly complex settings throughout their musical development.

In terms of tone quality, I incorporate *fundamental* and *explorative* strategies to assist students with their tonal awareness. Firstly, from a fundamental perspective of basic tone, I draw students' attention to the sound they make, what it means to listen, and how what we do with our body comes into play. Secondly, from an explorative perspective, I help students get familiar with exaggerated tone qualities, incorporating activities that promote tonal extremes and expand their tonal awareness. By exploring extremes and exaggerations, students develop a strengthening—a deep internalization—of tonal awareness and control. Extreme and exaggerated explorations function as the necessary and complementary tools in establishing the basics of tone and how the body produces it.

While it might seem like tone quality and rhythmic continuity are exclusively related to the body's physicality, that's not really the case. Here, it's also important to consider a complete range of emotional intensities, intellectual thought processes, intuitive understandings, and spiritual connections in regards to tonal and rhythmic awareness and control. Things such as: the disadvantages of teaching curved fingers and fixed body positions in contrast to the benefits of moving fingers, arm motions, and upper body flexibility; the advantage of getting off the bench and dancing; how tone production changes with emotional intensity; the danger of students thinking too much; what happens with letting go and being inside the performance; openness and trust as prerequisites to spiritual sensitivity. Through this multilayered and overlapping approach—physical, emotional, intellectual, intuitive, and spiritual—I purposely separate what the repertoire needs from what students need. I help students develop the competencies they'll need to perform the repertoire and beyond.

By differentiating between students' musical development and repertoire requirements, teachers may concentrate on whether students' competency is insufficient, sufficient, or more than sufficient to successfully perform the repertoire. Then, based on their observations, they address their students' needs by introducing appropriate follow up strategies. For example, when students' competency seems to be insufficient, teachers find out what's going on and why things might be missing from their teaching. When students' musical development appears sufficient, teachers explore how they got there, what they need to stay there, and how they might extend what's going on. When students' musical mastery seems to be more than sufficient, teachers challenge themselves and their students to find out what they might be taking for granted and what might happen if they went deeper. The advantage of teaching in this way is that no matter students' competency—insufficient, sufficient, or more than sufficient—the students' own development comes into play, not as fixed musical interpretations, but as ongoing and evolving processes of exploration and refinement.

6.2 Accumulated Repertoire, Review, and Refinement

Similar to the way children develop fluency in speaking through endless experimentation with their accumulated vocabulary, teachers may help students develop performance fluency through review and refinement of their accumulated repertoire. This means that instead of dropping pieces after they're learned, teachers encourage students to continue to refine the pieces they know how to play. They help students to internalize performance skills to a high degree of fluency so that when students start a new piece, they're able to incorporate their accumulated fluency rather than starting from scratch.

Traditionally, many studio music teachers use a process wherein students work on one piece at a time. Following successful performance of piece #1, students subsequently drop piece #1 in order to move on to piece #2 and they restart the process once again. In a similar manner, exam-based teachers may focus on four or five pieces for an entire year, with each year starting from a clean slate. The problem is that students may confidently perform their repertoire only for a brief time in contrast to the extended period they spend learning and refining before restarting the process with new repertoire. Students may actually spend less time at a high-level of mastery and more time on fixing undesirable performance traits or eliminating mistakes.

As an alternative, I propose using students' accumulated repertoire to facilitate review and refinement as the secure route to performance mastery. In an accumulated repertoire review/refinement approach, the first step of mastery is identical to the above traditional processes—teachers help students to learn, refine, and perform piece #1 over a period of time. However, rather than dropping piece #1 in order to move on to piece #2, teachers subsequently assist students with review/refinement of piece #1 while students add piece #2 to their repertoire. Teachers use review/refinement of students' successful accumulated repertoire as the secure building blocks for moving on to the next piece. Following students' successful performance of piece #2, teachers facilitate review/refinement of both pieces #1 and #2 while students add piece #3 to their repertoire, continuing in this manner until a reasonable number of pieces are accumulated. Using this approach, teachers not only reinforce and validate what students do well, but also deepen or broaden students' emergent fluency with tone quality and rhythmic continuity. They support students' competency as performers by developing consistency in students' musical achievements. As music education scholar Robert Duke affirmed in Intelligent Music Teaching (2005), because week after week teachers systematically guide students through the fundamentals of performance, the likelihood is high that students "will perform each component accurately and successfully" (p. 96).

> After approximately six months of piano lessons, Yumiko's accumulated repertoire consisted of ten beginner pieces. Every week, I heard all her pieces in order from the easiest and most fluent to her most recent and least fluent. On the occasions when Yumiko couldn't wait to show me her newest piece, I heard it first—knowing it would satisfy her need for recognition. Hearing Yumiko's accumulated repertoire in order every week meant that she could confidently anticipate the activities of each weekly lesson. She knew that we'd always begin by revisiting her successful repertoire, not in some kind of superficial replaying of pieces, but in a deliberate effort to create excellence in terms of concentration, piano tone and technique, and steady beat. To maintain Yumiko's interest in refining her accumulated repertoire, I made sure we had lots of fun coming up with challenges to engage her practice like playing with eyes closed, grabbing fingers, and no mistakes from beginning to end.
>
> In his third year of piano lessons, Joshua's accumulated repertoire consisted of six junior level pieces. Similar to Yumiko, I made sure to hear his entire accumulated repertoire at each lesson. However, for students at Joshua's level of study, I always begin with the newest piece. To maintain Joshua's interest in refining his accumulated repertoire, I encouraged a cyclical approach in which Joshua explored various themes like playing with dynamics, keeping the beat, arm freedom, playing my favorite way, playing Joshua's favorite way, and more.

This accumulated repertoire review/refinement approach has several benefits for students like Yumiko and Joshua. It means they may develop their fluency in repertoire they're most comfortable with. They develop the consistency in performance they'll need prior to learning their newest pieces. As the ratio between review/refinement pieces and brand new pieces increases, students spend more time enjoying fluent performances than struggling with unsuccessful explorations. It also means that Yumiko and Joshua always have lots of polished repertoire ready for impromptu performances, especially when relatives drop by for a visit or their schoolteachers make a performance request. That's why I fully encourage students to play a high number of review/refinement pieces during their home practices, knowing that they'll most likely find it more interesting to play a number of pieces rather than focus exclusively on refining one piece. What's key in an accumulated repertoire approach is that students have a manageable number of review/refinement pieces, that teachers prioritize students' engagement by assigning relevant and meaningful explorations, and that teachers provide follow up in each weekly lesson.

One of the questions teachers may ask regarding an accumulated repertoire instructional approach is—How can teachers possibly respond when students arrive with 10 pieces in one lesson? While this might seem impossible due to time restrictions, most beginner pieces are thirty seconds or less, so hearing 10 pieces is well within the limitations of a 30-minute lesson. This challenge is more likely related to students' independence and ownership (Chap. 2) of their successful performance and the possibility that on occasion they take ownership of errors or perform poorly. So, it's important for teachers to guide students in accurately recognizing their accomplishments because when teachers facilitate students' awareness of their own performances, teachers strengthen students' habits of fluency. They increase students' potential for a high proportion of success. This means that when students make errors or perform poorly, teachers need to figure out whether such inconsistencies are a reflection of an individual piece or group of pieces and respond appropriately. In this respect, there's no danger that students' errors will completely derail the positive impact of review/refinement.

An accumulated repertoire approach supports student growth by encouraging positive behaviors and productive awareness necessary for building students mastery of musicianship. Teachers who promote high amounts of successful performance naturally strengthen the consistency of students' fluency. How teachers choose to stimulate and support students' mastery of musicianship will determine the extent to which students successfully achieve the long-term goals of learning to play a musical instrument.

6.3 Teachers as Student Advocates

When teachers teach with an attitude of advocacy, they welcome students into unconditional learning processes that respect their personality, their home life, and their relentless desire for self-expression. Teachers provide leadership by bringing extensive knowledge and expertise to their instructional approach. However, developing student musicianship isn't about the teacher's journey. It's about the student's journey. Teaching with an attitude of advocacy means teachers appreciate who their students are. They trust what their students have to say—literally and musically. Teachers who advocate on their students' behalf accept and engage students for whom they genuinely are, not for whom teachers might want their students to be—as the following story demonstrates.

Five-year-old Benjamin has distinct preferences for slouching at the piano, moving around, and playing with a low wrist. He also has undeniably double-jointed fingers. My job is to guide Benjamin by getting to know who he is as a person and finding out how his worldview fits into learning to play the piano. That means every week, I check both his slouching and sitting tall, both moving around and not moving around, and both playing with a low and a not-low wrist—making sure Benjamin has opportunity to examine the positive or negative impact on his playing.

So, in my teaching, I advocate on my students' behalf. I stand up for their preferences while acknowledging that advocating doesn't mean I neutrally respond to whatever they have to offer. It means I incorporate teaching strategies that help them see beyond their own particular perspective.

6.4 Teachers as Student Agitators

In contrast to teachers who are student advocates, teachers as student agitators challenge their students by taking them just slightly beyond their comfort zone. They introduce explorations that break away from doing only what's easy, knowing that developing musicianship is a process that necessarily involves risk, instability, tension, and agitation.

Prominent educators have established a fundamental connection between educational processes and tension. The esteemed American education philosopher Dewey (1859–1952) describes how our thinking typically begins with what he terms a "felt difficulty", the interruptive occurrences that prompt us to search for solutions (1909, p. 72). He points out how our own doubt, perplexity, and mental difficulty serve as the stimulus for inquiry into material that will resolve doubts, settle and dispose of perplexity. In a similar vein, transformative education specialist Nadira Charaniya explains how learning processes are constantly being "formed and reformed through contact with the unexpected, the unfamiliar, and the challenging" (2012, p. 234). Learning experiences depend on teachers' and students' collaborative openness to the risks and tensions associated with new ideas and challenges. In this context, learning involves what might be referred to as acceptable tension—challenges that students feel are personally worthwhile, in contrast to challenges so hard that students cannot succeed, or so easy that students feel their time is wasted. As music education scholars Gembris and Davidson (2002) affirmed, "It is important for the child to always be sufficiently challenged and stretched without being overwhelmed or threatened" (p. 27).

Acceptable tension shows up in learning to play a musical instrument because successful, satisfying, or meaningful musical performances are not merely concerned with getting rid of tensions. Successful performances allow for, tap into, and generate the dynamic interplay of acceptable tensions comprising the performer's physical, emotional, intellectual, intuitive, and spiritual commitment to performance in juxtaposition with the musical score and the instrument's tonal temperament, not to mention the audience. The idea of acceptable tension sheds light on the fundamental characteristics of performance, often comprised of variable, changing, and oppositional elements such as feeling and thinking, tension and release, active and passive engagement, and impulsive and determined qualities.

Students may take on acceptable tensions because such challenges remind them of who they are (Chap. 2—authenticity). Manageable tensions and conflicts serve as intimate and fruitful avenues for exercising, experiencing, and exploring students' own sense of self. This is not to say that tensions and conflicts are the only avenues for meaningful personal exploration. Not in the least. Rather, that students' sense of authenticity is reaffirmed in their response to tensions and conflicts. Perhaps that's why students commonly introduce reasonable challenges like playing fast and loud as a way of testing or proving to themselves who they are as persons, as their own way of purposely demonstrating to teachers and parents the self-affirming value they derive from themselves.

With all levels of students, teachers may act as student agitators by incorporating such reasonable and manageable challenges as playing with eyes closed, playing without mistakes, and keeping a steady beat. When teachers agitate, they make sure students buy into the notion of challenging their own learning, and that students participate in actively stimulating their own musical development. This means some challenges have greater value than others, some have age-appropriate considerations, and others have limitations concerning the level of repertoire. And because tensions come in all sizes and shapes, certain reasonable conflicts and manageable discomforts may be worthy of attention, while the extremes of uninspiring and overly intense challenges may nullify and even extinguish student enthusiasm.

6.5 Caring for Music

As a musician, I confess to caring deeply about music. Caring seems to characterize my relationship with music because in many ways music seems to be part of who I am. So, it's not surprising that I was somewhat unprepared for the following conversation:

At nine years of age, Emily had been my piano student for five years, more than half of her entire life. In that time, I'd learned that if I was going to ask Emily a question, I needed to make sure it was one worth answering. So, after a particularly poor performance during her lesson, I took my time to find the right words.

> "Emily, why do you think sometimes kids play well and sometimes they
> don't?" I asked.
> Emily shrugged her shoulders. "Well... kids who play well, want to," she
> began. "And kids who don't, don't really care," followed by another shrug of
> her shoulders.
> I waited a moment before asking, "Could you play it with care?"

It's hard to believe that in all my years of piano teaching, studying the piano, having relationships, and observing people, it never dawned on me that not really caring about how something turned out could have such an obvious outcome. Of course, it made sense that if people did not care whether they play well or not that it would show up in their performance. The solution to Emily not playing well, as it turned out, was as direct as my initial question.

When I asked Emily to share her thoughts, I must admit that I was anticipating something quite different. After five years of piano lessons, I expected her to answer with any number of informed responses having to do with accurate notes, rhythmic consistency, or tone quality. Emily responded to my impromptu inquiry with remarkable insight, even though such questions can easily be dismissed by mechanical answers that focus on anticipating what the teacher wants to hear, rather than what both student and teacher are searching to discover or explore. I never expected that her answer would call upon the notion of caring.

Nel Noddings, Stanford University education professor, has written extensively on the notion of care and its importance to education. In her works on care theory (2005, 2010), Noddings describes how human beings are born into relationships, how our original condition is one of relations with others. However, this doesn't mean that human beings are universally predisposed to care for others—in fact, she acknowledges how anthropologists have identified various social groups where caring is not evident. In contrast, Noddings claims that people everywhere have a predisposition or desire to being cared-for by others, a tendency that human beings instinctively seek out for themselves. This desire to be cared-for is built into humanity as a kind of primal element that varies between individuals and from one life stage to another. By underscoring the distinction between being cared-for and caring, Noddings draws attention to the fundamental difference between receiving care and giving care, and how actively caring may require a significant shifting away from the individually-centered desire to be cared-for.

In the context of students learning to play a musical instrument, it's interesting to consider Nodding's distinction between being cared-for and caring. Being cared-for refers to the ways in which students receive care from music, whereas caring refers to students' active participation in caring for music. In being cared-for by music, students encounter the welcomed experiences of personal gratification, joy, comfort, ease, release, and distraction associated with music. Whether it's through listening to music, imagining a musical motif, performance on an instrument, or playing around with sound, musical explorations possess vitality capable of satisfying students' desire to be cared-for. Students enjoy musical explorations and appreciate having music in their lives because of the way music makes them feel. The safety and security associated with being cared-for may make it challenging for students to actively shift into caring for music. Students may be so comfortable with being cared-for by the vitality of music that they fail to recognize their role in caring for music. Noddings provides a solution to shifting from being cared-for to caring by emphasizing that becoming "prepared to care requires practice" (2010, p. 395).

As an aspect of teaching students, it seems I owe a great deal of gratitude to my student Emily for her insight into caring. Her awareness of caring has a lot in common with Noddings' proposition that students must be given opportunities to care. When students practice caring for music, their concern shifts from fulfilling their own self-interests to consider the wellbeing of music. Their relationship with music develops a reciprocity guided by the inherent needs of the musical performance in relation to students' values, the resources available, and students' competency. Caring for music requires students to continually practice as the means to developing increased competency necessary for responding to the breadth of musical explorations. It's an aspect of teaching students vital to every teacher's instructional strategy.

6.6 Final Thoughts

Having examined various themes associated with what it means to teach students, it occurs to me that teaching students places enormous demands on teachers' knowledge and expertise. From one perspective, teachers need to know how to separate student needs from repertoire needs as the prerequisite for helping students explore the fundamentals of musical self-expression: tone quality and rhythmic continuity. From another perspective, teachers need to know where students are headed, how they're going to help students get there, how they'll strengthen and promote students' ongoing mastery of musicianship. Then, there's the perspective involved in moving back and forth between advocating and agitating on behalf of students, knowing when to support and protect in contrast to those days when it's vital for teachers to challenge students in stepping outside their own comfort zone. Finally, teaching students means being attentive to the aspect of receiving and giving care, taking the time to recognize what music brings to our lives and what music requires from each of us.

The purpose of teaching students through musical explorations may be defined in terms of giving spark to the flame that is the child's sense of self. Teachers use music making as the resonant avenue for exercising, exploring, and experiencing a flourishing of their students. They make teaching their students a priority. And by putting students at the center of teaching, teachers foster the student's sense of self. Quite remarkably through the circuitous journey of musical studies, improvisations, achievements, and frustrations, teachers help their students get a particular picture of who they are. Teachers reinforce their students' sense of self in the ways they make music—whether it's out-of-control fast and loud, or the loving expressions of emotional mastery. Through the purposeful and sometimes fleeting moments of teaching and learning, musical explorations remind each of us about who we are. And in this dynamic environment, teachers have not only the responsibility of sharing their musical experiences, they also have the immense privilege of listening to what students have to say as active music makers in the resonating world of music.

6.7   Before We Move on

1. This chapter explored what's involved in teaching students as different from teaching repertoire. How would you assess your own autobiographical musical development in terms of these contrasting ideas? Do you see more of one approach than the other? Which one? Why do you think your previous music teachers might have preferred one approach over the other?
2. How do you feel about your ability to separate repertoire needs from student needs? Do you have a preference? How can you strengthen your capacity for developing students' musicianship?
3. The aspect of using students' accumulated repertoire as the foundation for musical development is typically missing from traditional and exam-based approaches. What is your own experience with using accumulated repertoire to build musical mastery? How might you incorporate this idea into your own teaching?
4. Teachers bring support and challenges as advocates and agitators to their students' musical development. How have these two aspects been part of your own musical autobiography? In your own teaching, which do you prefer to do? How might you incorporate both of these strategies with your students?
5. Caring for music seems to be integral to a musician's relationship with music. How can you include this aspect in your teaching without diminishing your students' desire for playing around or doodling with music?

References

Camp, M. (1981). *Developing piano performance: A teaching philosophy.* Chapel Hill, NC: Hinshaw Music.
Caposey, P. J. (2014). *Teach smart: 11 learner-centered strategies that ensure student success.* New York, NY: Routledge.

Charaniya, N. K. (2012). Cultural-spiritual perspective of transformative learning. In E. Taylor & P. Cranton (Eds.), *The handbook of transformative learning*. San Francisco, CA: Jossey-Bass.

Davis, B., Sumara, D., & Luce-Kapler, R. (2015). *Engaging minds: Cultures of education and practices of teaching* (3rd ed.). New York, NY: Routledge.

Dewey, J. (1909). *How we think*. Boston, MA: D.C. Heath.

Duke, R. (2005). *Intelligent music teaching*. Austin, TX: Learning and Behavior Resources.

Gembris, H., & Davidson, J. (2002). Environmental influences. In R. Parncutt & G. McPherson (Eds.), *The science and psychology of music performance* (pp. 17–30). Oxford, UK: Oxford University Press.

Neuhaus, H. (1973). *The art of piano playing* (Trans. K. Leibovitch). Wolfeboro, NH: Longwood Academic.

Noddings, N. (2005). *The challenge to care in schools: An alternative approach to education*. New York, NY: Teachers College Press.

Noddings, N. (2010). Moral education in an era of globalization. *Educational Philosophy and Theory, 42*(4), 390–396.

Weimer, M. (2013). *Learner-centered teaching: Five key changes to practice (2nd ed.)*. Jossey-Bass.

Whiteside, A. (1961). *Indispensables of piano playing*. New York, NY: Coleman-Ross.

Chapter 7
Taking Parents into Consideration

Abstract Researchers have repeatedly affirmed that parental interest in their children's musical development has a noticeably positive impact on children's musical development even without parents having any musical knowledge. Knowing that parents and teachers naturally bring different yet overlapping perspectives to beginner piano students, this chapter considers the relation between teachers and parents. An examination of interactions between teachers and parents from a historical perspective and within musical settings reveals that teachers may unconsciously perpetuate attitudes of assumed authority over parents. As an alternative, teachers may establish meaningful parent relations by developing openness and trust that includes listening to what parents have to contribute, figuring out what they need, finding out what works, and drawing from what's already there rather than trying to reconfigure the family's structure. This chapter concludes by providing practical information for the first conversation with parents, musical cornerstones for parents, welcoming real life families, and twice-yearly teacher-parent interviews.

Students seldom learn to play a musical instrument in isolation, even though they may spend considerable amounts of time practicing on their own. They're greatly influenced by their surrounding musical resources: the musical input of their teachers, the performance models of other students, their access to recordings, youtube videos, and concerts. Most importantly, there is widespread agreement in education research regarding an additional influence on students' musical development—that is parental interest—the unconditional and supportive way parents engage with their children.[1] Researchers have affirmed that young children and adolescents alike experience improved musical development when parents take an interest in what they're doing, even without any musical knowledge on the part of the parent. In other words, it's not what parents know about music that's most valuable—it's the loving relationship parents have with their children that has the greatest impact.

---

[1]On the influence of parental interest and support see: Bloom (1985), Creech (2009), Davidson et al. (1995), Gonzalez-DeHass et al. (2005), Sloboda (1993), Stitt and Brooks (2014).

© The Author(s) 2018   75
M.B. Thompson, *Fundamentals of Piano Pedagogy*,
SpringerBriefs in Education, DOI 10.1007/978-3-319-65533-8_7

With unconditional love at the core of parents' relationships with their child, it's as if parents can't resist taking an interest in their child's development. They exclaim with delight at the child's first words and steps. They validate children's efforts to feed themselves, get dressed, play with toys, communicate, or show affection for others. Through loving interactions with their child, parents develop unmatched knowledge and insight into their child as a person. No other person knows that child in the fundamental way parents know their child. Not grandparents, in-laws, or teachers, because parents know their child from the fullness of daily life rather than from a distance, a temporary outing, or an optimal occasion. No matter the child's temperament, age, personality, strengths or weaknesses, parents know what it means to provide loving support for their child under all kinds of circumstances. They create the dynamic conditions for supporting their child's independent desire to explore the world and learn things like playing a musical instrument. They provide confirmation of their child as an independent learner and a hope for their child's better life.

This confirmation of independence, learning, and hope bears remarkable similarities to the results of an investigation by the American career analyst Pink. In his 2009 book *Drive: The Surprising Truth About What Motivates Us*, Pink makes an outstanding observation that satisfaction in life is rooted in the deeply human need to direct our own lives, to learn and create new things, and to do better by ourselves and our world. Although Pink's target audience is neither children learning to play a musical instrument nor their parents, his remarks bring a kind of eloquent illumination to the message behind parents' loving interest for their child. Parents take an interest in their child because they recognize their child's satisfaction in life, similar to Pink, is bound to the child's closely-held need to direct his or her own life, to learn and create, and to live with meaning and purpose.

Long before children begin music lessons, parents may support their child's natural inclination towards independence, learning, and engaging with purpose. They take an interest in their child's endeavors because, on the one hand, they know the joy, the inexplicable empowerment, and magical sense of satisfaction that comes with meaningful independent exploration. On the other hand, parents also know what it's like to have independence taken away, to be denied opportunities to learn, and to have their meaningful endeavors go unrecognized. So, it's only natural that parents would want to motivate and validate their child's experience of independence, learning and creating, and doing things with purpose and meaning. Even though, as parenting author Coloroso affirmed, some parents may interpret their role in terms of "an obsession with order, control, and obedience, a rigid adherence to rules, and a strict hierarchy of power" (1995, p. 40).

When children start music lessons, it's important for teachers to remember that parents already have a supportive relationship with their child. They've not only witnessed their child's inclination for independent learning, they've also actively motivated and validated their child's accomplishments. Knowing that parents and teachers naturally bring different yet overlapping perspectives to the child's process of learning to play a musical instrument, the question is—What does parental involvement look like and how might teachers support parents in this matter? This chapter examines the relation between teachers and parents from various angles.

7.1 Historical Implications

Parents and teachers share a primary bond, not to each other, but to the children whose lives they strive to improve and inspire. For parents, their child may be the most important person in their lives, the one who arouses their deepest passions and stimulates their fiercest advocacy and protection. And it is teachers—those knowledgeable and experienced adults—to whom parents turn to enrich and extend their children's lives. Parents seek out teachers' advice and guidance because they recognize that teachers may facilitate processes that speed up children's learning process, assisting children in making positive changes to their own knowledge and expertise. Parents include teachers in their children's lives, intuitively recognizing that teachers occupy a lasting and honorable social status because of their expertise in the arts, mathematics, sports, science, and more. In this respect, there's something trusting and admirable about the interactions between parents and teachers.

During the past several hundred years in Western Europe and North America, the dialogue between parents and teachers has experienced significant fluctuations as tempered by cultural, institutional, educational, economic, and historical forces. Prior to the late 1800s, parents in upper and middle class households took charge of their children's education, whereas working class and poor parents were not equipped to provide for their children's education due to unstable work conditions and the family's reliance on children as economic contributors. However, with the introduction of compulsory public schools in the 1880s, teachers took on an official capacity as experts with respect to issues of education and child development both inside and outside of schools. Social reformers and educators asserted that parents could not adequately provide for their children's educational needs without expert intervention. So, parents were purposely kept at a distance from the responsibility of educating their children and teachers were placed in a position of power (Tutwiler 2005, p. 18). Interaction between teachers and parents during the era from 1880 to 1920, as described by the American educational authority Wallis (1899–1945) in his book *The Sociology of Teaching* (1932), was all about teachers getting "parents to see children more or less as teachers see them" (p. 69).

Groundbreaking developments during the twentieth century had a noticeable impact on parents and teachers. The women's suffragette movement, increased educated women, falling birthrates, and women working outside the home—these factors all had an evolving effect on women's parenting role. Childrearing practices following World War II, spurred by the advice of child experts such as Dr. Spock (1946), encouraged parents to move away from authoritarian parenting and trust their own instincts and common sense, to be openly affectionate with their children, and to treat their children as individuals. The Civil Rights movement, feminist movement, and sexual revolution of the 1960s brought about changes in attitudes towards racial equality, reproductive choice, and the emergence of gay and lesbian rights. Resulting from this period of phenomenal change and the educational challenges facing children, governmental institutions in Europe and North America recognized the need for parents to be more directly involved in the education of their children (Tutwiler 2005, p. 106). From the 1980s onward, educational organizations responded with strategies aimed at reducing the distance between schools and families by encouraging parents' involvement in their children's education. Expressions highlighting parental 'participation', 'partnerships', 'involvement', and 'community' during this period are noteworthy because, as education researcher Vincent (1996) pointed out, these words may obscure more than they illuminate. Such expressions evoke positive images of respectful interaction while camouflaging the hierarchical imbalance between teachers and parents. Many teachers continue to adhere to a mindset that places parents in a "subordinate position in relation to the professionals" (Vincent 1996, p. 149). Teachers view parental support as all about parents assimilating teachers' values and behaviors, deeming good parents as those who defer to the school and the professional claims of its teachers.

Over the course of the twentieth century, the interaction between parents and teachers evolved gradually starting with distancing parents from their child's education during the advent of compulsory public schools in comparison to the more recent language of teacher-directed partnership and participation. However throughout this developmental process, the dialogue between parents and teachers demonstrates a singular consistent characteristic—namely, that teachers' attitude of hierarchical authority remains unchanged. What I find fascinating is how this historical legacy seems to position teachers as social authorities whose expertise allowed them to define the parameters of raising children both in terms of education and parenting.

7.2 Teachers and Parents in Musical Settings

In literature related to music instruction, the dialogue between teachers and parents demonstrates remarkable similarities to the hierarchical interaction of teachers and parents in public education. Beginning with Matthay's book on piano teaching (1913), we may interpret Matthay's omission of the subject of parents as in keeping with the distancing practice of the early 1900s. During the 1950s, music teachers maintained their position of authority while demonstrating a superficial awareness of parents and a subtle disregard for interactions with parents. In an example from *The Young Pianist: A New Approach for Teachers and Students* (1954), Last described parents in exasperating terms—"What a help *or* hindrance they can be!" (p. 4). Acknowledging the "cooperation of parents is essential", she suggested:

> It is a good plan for the mother to attend an occasional lesson to see how the child should sit, and to get an idea of the work that is being done. These attendances should not be too frequent as children are usually much easier to teach when mother is not there (pp. 5–6).

Although Last recommended teachers "have as close an understanding with the parents as possible" (p. 6), it seems she preferred to keep parents at a distance and regards their input as intrusive. Her authoritarian tone indicated an overt marginalizing of parents.

Ahrens and Atkinson, pedagogy experts at the Royal Conservatory of Music in Toronto, portrayed a similar indifference while keeping parents at a distance consistent with a hierarchical teacher approach in *For All Piano Teachers* (1955).

> In the earliest stages of a child's music study some sort of supervision of his practicing is almost a necessity. The mother, an older brother or sister, or even a friend of the family may appear in the role of supervisor. Such supervision must be under the direction of the teacher, and would cease as soon as the child may safely be left to himself (p. 48).

During the 1960s and 1970s, music teachers modified their interaction with parents through documents focused primarily on sharing information. For example, in *A Parent's Guide to Music Lessons* (1966), Egbert enlightens parents with a three-page article of insights into learning to play a musical instrument. Ten years later, the amount of parental information needed to support their child increased dramatically with a publication by Bastien, Notre Dame piano faculty member. His 70-page book *A Parent's Guide to Piano Lessons* (1976) aimed to assist parents with helping the "child get as much out of piano lessons as possible" (p. 3). While these documents have immense practicality as sources of information, they contain a subtle underlying message—that teachers prefer parents to view their child's musical studies from the teacher's perspective. As music educator Rabin affirmed in her book *At the Beginning: Teaching Piano to the Very Young Child* (1996), parents are the teachers' "eyes and ears at home" (p. 23). Interestingly, Rabin incorporates the language of parents as "partners" (p. 25) evident in the public school setting while ensuring parents occupy a subordinate position that serves teachers' authoritarian stance.

Moving to the twenty-first century, there is a trend among music teachers to define parental involvement through a language of clearly formalized parental responsibilities that may include: provide a piano, pay tuition, get the child to lessons on time, take notes at the lesson, assist the child with home practice, check lesson assignments, make sure all materials are practiced, and complete the practice chart. An example of parental responsibilities contained in a one-page framework by piano pedagogue Jacobson (2006) comprises 21 parent responsibilities, 7 student responsibilities, and 11 teacher responsibilities—a simple calculation reveals that parents have triple the responsibilities of their children and double the responsibilities of teachers in ensuring a "level of success in each student's progress" (p. 363). While there are obvious benefits for parents to provide a piano, pay tuition, and be actively involved with their children's musical development, this emphasis on parental responsibilities bears a strong resemblance to the historical requirement for parents to assimilate teachers' values and behaviors in order to replicate the teacher's perspective.

Another aspect evident in formalized parental involvement strategies has to do with how teachers prefer to communicate with parents. While there is general agreement in the literature on the importance of communication with parents, it often comes across as a one-way street. For example, music educator Fisher (2010) suggested teachers provide parents with "written evaluations of student progress on a regular basis", but gives no opportunity for parental input despite the requirement of parents' active involvement in attending lessons and practising with their child (pp. 181–184). Jacobson (2006) proposed teachers formalize how they prefer to handle problems that may arise. She encourages parents to contact the teacher immediately if they perceive problems and to keep in close contact during office hours from 10:00 a.m. to noon, specifically avoiding discussion of problematic areas before, during, or after their child's lesson (p. 362). So, at first glance, it seems teachers respectfully acknowledge problems may arise and are generous in offering their time for discussion. However, when we look more closely, there is a somewhat hidden message that parental awareness of problems and their need for solutions is secondary to the teacher's agenda. No matter how actively parents are involved at home or attentive in their child's lesson, the hierarchical position of teachers' goals and focus on students during the lesson period must always take priority over parental input.

Despite the teacher-centered nature of recent formalized interactions between parents and music teachers, many parents succeed in supporting their children's musical development, even when they don't regularly check their child's lesson assignments or fill out practice charts. What seems to be missing from the above studio music settings is the acknowledgement that parents bring their own highly relevant perspectives to children's musical studies, they bring practical concerns and hopeful aspirations for their children. Most significantly, parents also implicitly and explicitly convey personal philosophies and attitudes. They reveal themselves in conversations with their child, in their responses to music, and in the stories they tell about themselves, their children, music, education, and life (Thompson 2016b).

7.3 Meaningful Conversations

In her book *The Essential Conversation* (2003), Harvard University sociologist Sara Lawrence-Lightfoot suggests that teachers need to become skilled at "joining forces with parents on behalf of children" in order to build collaborative and authentic relationships with the families of their students (pp. 227–228). She highlights how teachers who see parents as the child's first educators are respectful of their experience and perspective, and listen carefully to their observations and insights about their children. Under such circumstances, parents and teachers respect and value what the other knows and brings to the child's experience of learning. They're appreciative of and empathetic towards each other, not as some sort of gushing sentimentality, but in terms of walking in the other person's shoes and seeing the world from the other person's vantage point. In contrast to the hierarchical teacher practices described above, Lawrence-Lightfoot's ideas stand as a reminder for teachers to truly understand how other people lead their lives, how parents and teachers bring overlapping yet necessarily different perspectives to the education of children.

Music teachers may make meaningful connections between what happens in the lesson to what's already going on at home by getting to know parents and understanding how parents contribute to their child's learning. This means teachers recognize and acknowledge that parents bring their own personal knowledge, life experiences, expertise, lifestyle, and expectations to their child's musical explorations. Teachers comfortable with this kind of parental interaction operate as collaborative communicators equally skilled in listening and responding sensitively to parents. American educator Rudney (2005) suggested, teachers may create positive relationships with parents by asking "not what parents can do for them, but rather what they can do for parents" (p. 50). In this context, teachers aren't afraid that parental input might derail their vision of music instruction; rather, they recognize that good communication is a two-way street and that understanding what parents need and want is vital.

One of the images Lawrence-Lightfoot used to describe the dialogue between parents and teachers is that of "neighbors chatting over the back fence" (2003, p. 245). When neighbors chat over the fence, there's a friendliness and comfort to their conversations about topics of mutual concern and interest. They share enough information to get a sense of each other, without soliciting or sharing so much information that it becomes intrusive or uncomfortable. Chatting over the back fence signals an openness to look out for each other's wellbeing and an anticipation of living side-by-side for years to come.

I appreciate the image of neighbors chatting because conversations aren't just about what one person has to say. Conversations aren't about teachers controlling what parents do, nor for that matter, parents dictating to teachers. Similar to the mutual concerns and interests between neighbors, meaningful conversations between parents and teachers share a focus on the best interests of the child learning to play a musical instrument. There's a back and forth quality to chatting over the fence that highlights how parents and teachers both contribute to children's musical studies. They both have something to say while, similar to neighbors honoring the fence that separates them, there's respect for each other's boundaries. Fruitful discussions aren't about taking over each other's lives in some sort of hierarchical positioning of power. Both parents and teachers bring something vital to children's musical explorations.

In my own teaching, I like to think my interactions with parents have a lot in common with Lawrence-Lightfoot's conversations over the back fence. From my first informal conversation with new parents to the twice-yearly formal parent-teacher interviews, helping families means recognizing where they already are and figuring out what they'll need from me.

7.3.1   Teachers' First Encounter with Parents

For most piano teachers, the first encounter with parents typically occurs when parents inquire via telephone or email into music lessons for their child. As this initial inquiry has the potential to either encourage or dissuade parents from further involvement, it seems paramount that teachers communicate their ability and readiness for guiding students' future musical development. This can be especially challenging given that parents' rationale for music lessons may cover a complete spectrum as the following scenarios demonstrate.

Parent A   "I just want my child to have fun in learning to play the piano. We're going to give it a try for two years and if it's not fun, we'll move on to another activity."

Parent B   "My child has a lot of difficulty with concentration. So I think the discipline of learning the piano would be very beneficial."

Parent C   "I want my child to complete upper level RCM examinations for extra credit in high school. That will be our primary goal for learning to play the piano."

So, how can teachers respond when parental expectations do not match the teacher's philosophy or goals? Would the teacher be wise to suggest that another teacher might better meet their needs? What kind of communication is appropriate?

Several years ago, I conducted a workshop on communication for studio music teachers. When I asked the participants to describe the attributes of effective communicators, they all agreed effective communicators possess two vitally interdependent skills: the skill of listening and the skill of speaking. However, when I asked them to use the skills of listening and speaking to respond to the above scenarios, I discovered they had very different definitions of listening and speaking from my own. They all thought teachers needed to listen carefully so they could come up with compelling arguments that would point out limitations of the parents' viewpoint. Whereas, I thought listening carefully meant developing an understanding of parents so that teachers might build on—rather than tear down—the parents' viewpoint.

Although each of the above scenarios isolates a particular aspect of learning to play the piano, what's remarkable is how each one provides sufficient reason for parents to enroll their child in music lessons. So, how can teachers realistically respond in a manner that respects the parents' viewpoint without relinquishing their own teaching philosophy? My immediate response to parents is always, "That's a great starting point", knowing that the complexity of my teaching draws from all of the above parental perspectives and more. By acknowledging the parents' viewpoint, I get things underway with parental support instead of minimizing their intentions. Subsequently as their child's musicianship develops, I make sure to point out how my instruction ties into parents' viewpoint while shedding light on aspects of musical development parents may not have anticipated. I don't give up my teaching philosophy to accommodate the parents' rationale; rather, I use the parents' viewpoint as the fertile ground for cultivating a broad spectrum of long-term musical growth.

7.3.2 Real Life Families

Whether parents attend their child's lessons and practise with their child at home is a matter that deserves flexibility and understanding from teachers. I want to be sure parents understand that learning to play a musical instrument isn't about parents sacrificing themselves to meet the needs of their child or their child's teacher. Because teachers have the knowledge and expertise necessary to create success under multiple conditions, they can respond effectively to a wide variety of family situations. As education expert Rudney (2005) stated, "Families come in different shapes and sizes" (p. 60). This means it's up to teachers to get to know their families so their teaching has meaningful connections with what's going on and what's possible at home.

The Robinson family schedule was complex. The Mother had her own medical practice; the Father worked in construction. So, they regularly enlisted their children's Grandmother's assistance. Every week, I never knew who would bring the children for their lessons—Mother, Father, or Grandmother? For the children, it was extraordinarily motivational to have the support of three adults. As the children's piano teacher, I became the consistent conduit, making sure Mother, Father, and Grandmother could understand and appreciate everything that was going on. My responsibility to the Robinsons was all about figuring out what they needed from me, finding out what worked, and drawing from what was already there, rather than trying to reconfigure their family structure.

In my own teaching, I find the weekly student lesson has great practicality for sharing information with parents. However, to be clear—I'm not looking for parents to duplicate the teacher's role in their own home; nor, do I spend voluminous amounts of time talking to parents. Rather, my goal is to demystify learning to play a musical instrument by succinctly connecting my instruction to parents' knowledge and life experiences. My role is similar to a musical tour guide who expeditiously reinforces what makes sense and proactively clarifies what might seem completely mindboggling for parents, knowing that unexplained occurrences and unresolved issues can easily make parents uncomfortable.

7.3.3 Input from Parents Is Vital

Parents see their children every day, while teachers see their students once a week. So, it makes sense for parents and teachers to depend on each other's input—not just in discussions about problem areas. They rely on each other to meaningfully share what's working, to ask the questions that need answering, to be reasonable and respectful of each other's values, life experiences, and expectations.

Given that I welcome parental input as part of our ongoing dialogue, parents frequently have things to share at the beginning or during their child's lessons. In particular, they may want me to know about their family's challenges at home. My response is to always listen respectfully, knowing that parents may be looking for my assistance in resolving their challenges or they may simply want me to be aware of and to acknowledge their concerns. Either way, this kind of immediate parental input is vital for my teaching to resonate with what's going on in the child's home. For teachers who think the lesson period is exclusively reserved for interaction with their students and that parents should attend as silent observers, this type of interaction with parents may seem completely out of line. However, my impression is that parents' input and need for clarification go hand in hand with effective teaching.

With meaningful and at times spur-of-the-moment dialogue between parents and teachers, music teaching connects with the realities of family life. Although phone calls or appointments at a later date may work, such policies seem to be more about keeping parents at a distance than welcoming parents with timely information and support. The five to six minutes I might devote to parents during their child's thirty-minute lesson are a modest investment in making sure that my teaching compliments the real life goings-on of my students' families.

7.3.4 Musical Cornerstones

My job is to make sure parents know about the two music-related cornerstones they can put in place to stimulate and support their child's musical development. The first cornerstone is listening to repertoire recordings because with adequate listening, children take ownership of learning to play by ear. Without it, independent music learning is in jeopardy. Playing the recording is an easy thing for parents to do that may empower their child's independence. The second cornerstone of independence is practising. I encourage parents to be motivators and validators of their child's independent learning experiences, to take a genuine interest in their child's efforts as emerging musicians because children who take ownership of their musical progress develop the skills, knowledge, and confidence necessary to go on to the next level of study. In other words, the more parents support their child's accomplishments as an independent learner; the sooner children make genuine progress on their own.

"How do you feel about Jason being an independent musician from today onward?" I asked Mr. Zhang, the Father of six-year-old beginner Jason.
"Well, that would be great, but is it really possible from today onward?" he replied, somewhat doubtfully.
"Actually it is," I affirmed. "By playing Jason's repertoire CD, you can help him get the pieces in his ears before he explores them at the piano. Just like listening to you speak Chinese has influenced Jason's learning to speak Chinese. For Jason, learning to play by ear will definitely impact his independence."

For beginner piano students, the more parents support their child's efforts in learning by ear; the sooner children will be able to play by ear and subsequently move on to learning by reading. Helping children to develop independent learning skills while being supported by parents makes it easier for parents to become progressively less involved in their child's learning.

Parents' support isn't a lifelong commitment to direct parental involvement—rather, as children grow in knowledge and sophistication, interaction with their parents naturally changes. This sheds light on age-related considerations, given that support for a beginning preschool child differs from support for an elementary school child or a teenager. How parents show support and interact with their child gradually evolves from direct and indirect participation with preschool children, to guiding and stepping away from school-age students, and finally, to being supportive and interested in what independent adolescent music students are going through.

For students of all ages, parental support regarding a consistent practice routine is often most beneficial, although some students may long for unfiltered, creative experimentations. This aspect of parental involvement has immense significance in view of research by music education scholars McPherson and Davidson (2006) who revealed that most parents stop reminding their child to practice at the time when their child most needs to be reminded. Whereas parents may continue to remind their child to do his or her academic homework for however many years it takes, parents frequently withdraw their support from their child's musical studies (p. 344). They seem to believe that children genuinely connected to music will spontaneously and independently invest the appropriate personal time and effort. A 2005 YouGov survey of 2000 respondents, undertaken by the Music Industries Association in Great Britain, found that 73% of respondents regretted giving up playing a musical instrument (Hallam and Creech 2010, p. 85). Unfortunately, hindsight is usually 20/20 in that many adults wish their parents had made them continue practising. Fortunately, parents' interest and support may significantly contribute to their children's ability to successfully overcome the recurring challenges of practising and following teachers' instructions associated with learning to play a musical instrument.

7.3.5 Parent-Teacher Interviews

In her work with parents, Nova Scotia teacher Baskwill (1989) described parents as wanting to "become involved in their children's learning and ensure their success… They have a wealth of information about their children to share" (p. 61). So, it's important for teachers to structure their teaching in ways that allow them to not only communicate informally with parents and also welcome formal parental input along the way (Thompson 2015). I want to tap into the vast knowledge of life and relationships that parents bring to their child's growth.

One of the ways I incorporate ongoing formal parental input is through 15-minute parent-teacher interviews that take place the final weeks of December and May of each year. During the week of parent-teacher interviews, I don't teach any lessons, knowing that families already have enough to do without making two trips to my studio. Prior to the interviews, I fill out a report card for each of my students that addresses the following: Study habits, Technical development, Reading development, Self expression, Attitude, Events attended, and General progress (Thompson 2014). Report cards help me monitor what I'm doing as a teacher, providing opportunity to identify areas I may consistently and inconsistently address. Because I keep previous and current report cards, I can get a clear idea of what's working and what needs extra attention or a different approach at the individual student's level. Parent-teacher interviews provide a highly valuable and essential opportunity to find out what parents think I need to know about their child.

> After examining and talking through their child's report card, I typically ask parents, "What do you need from me?" I like asking this question because it reinforces how much I value their knowledge and experience and how much I value being part of their child's musical development. So, I naturally want to find out how my teaching supports their child's growth. I welcome parental input because I realize they have their own insight into what's working, into what I might possibly do differently, and areas that I might never have considered on my own.

Of course, I realize that many teachers may be uncomfortable with the idea of asking for parental input. What if parents don't like what the teacher is doing? My response is that when parents and teachers aren't on the same page in terms of a child's development, it's better to find out sooner than later. Sooner means that teachers can do something about it. Later ultimately means it's the child that suffers. That's why I remain purposefully invitational, recognizing that although my role is to provide musical and instructional leadership, I am in this role at the parents' request. I set up an attitude of openness and reciprocal trust where it's not about rolling out my own agenda, nor parents running the show. It's about genuinely listening to each other.

7.4 Final Thoughts

As a child, I attended twelve years of piano lessons all on my own. During that time, I have scant memories of my parents ever talking with my piano teachers. On occasion, they had obligatory rushed conversations following performances, but other than that, it seems my parents had very little connection to my instructors. So, when I began teaching piano at the McGill Conservatory in the late 1970s, I wasn't entirely certain how to welcome parents into my studio. Yet, in looking back on three decades of my career, it's easy to see how working with entire families has influenced my teaching. In particular, I've learned that parents can depend on me to create a successful and meaningful learning environment, to sensitively and practically respond to their family's potentials and limitations.

Parents have multiple obligations. They have jobs, partner needs, laundry, making meals, housekeeping, planning for next year and the next ten years. While parents have astounding amounts of life experience to draw from in supporting their child's musical explorations, unfortunately, the distractions and conflicts of daily life can easily disrupt their efforts. At times, it's as if parents have a million things on their minds. This means that parental involvement in their child's learning doesn't take place in some kind of idyllic fantasy setting. It takes place within the hectic schedule of daily life.

For teachers, recognizing real life parents means welcoming their strengths and obstacles, rather than attempting to mold them into a teacher's dream version of parents. Teachers have the responsibility of opening doors for parents, to introduce parents to meaningful ways of thinking about teaching and learning (Thompson 2016a). It's up to teachers to make personal connections with parents' ideologies, attitudes, and philosophies—to link with the expansive resource that is what parents already know about life. In this respect, teachers become a conduit for generous and open explorations into the meaning of relationships, the fundamentals of learning, the impact of music, and more.

7.5 Before We Move on

1. What are some examples of your own parents' influence on your musical development until now? What do you appreciate about your parents' involvement? What might they have done differently?
2. Teachers may create positive relationships with parents by asking "not what parents can do for them, but rather what they can do for parents". How do you feel about this statement?

3. Teachers and parents may have very different ideas related to learning to play a musical instrument. How may teachers respectfully acknowledge the differences and similarities between parents' and teachers' perspectives concerning children and music lessons?
4. What do you think is essential for parents to know about learning to play a musical instrument? How and when may teachers convey this information to parents?
5. Conversations between teachers and parents may occur both formally and informally. What kind of formal interactions are part of your teaching routine? How do informal interactions contribute to parent/teacher relations?

References

Ahrens, C., & Atkinson, G. (1955). *For all piano teachers*. Oakville, ON: Frederick Harris Music Co.

Baskwill, J. (1989). *Parents and teachers: Partners in learning*. Toronto, ON: Scholastic.

Bastien, J. W. (1976). *A parent's guide to piano lessons*. San Diego, CA: Kjos West.

Bloom, B. (1985). *Developing talent in young people*. New York, NY: Ballantine Books.

Coloroso, B. (1995). *Kids are worth it*. Toronto, ON: Somerville House Publishing.

Creech, A. (2009). The role of the family in supporting learning. In S. Hallam & I. T. Cross (Eds.), *The Oxford handbook of music psychology* (pp. 295–3006). Oxford, UK: Oxford University Press.

Davidson, J., Howe, M., & Sloboda, J. (1995). The role of parents in the success and failure of instrumental learners. *Bulletin of the Council for Research in Music Education, 127,* 40–44.

Egbert, M. S. (1966, March). A parent's guide to piano lessons. *Music Journal*.

Fisher, C. (2010). *Teaching piano in groups*. New York, NY: Oxford University Press.

Gonzalez-DeHass, A., Willems, P., & Doan Holbein, M. (2005). Examining the relationship between parental involvement and student motivation. *Educational Psychology Review, 17,* 99–123.

Hallam, S., & Creech, A. (2010). *Music education in the 21st century in the United Kingdom*. London, UK: Institute of Education Press.

Jacobson, J. (2006). *Professional piano teaching*. Los Angeles, CA: Alfred Publishing.

Last, J. (1954). *The young pianist: A new approach for teachers and students*. London, UK: Oxford University Press.

Lawrence-Lightfoot, S. (2003). *The essential conversation*. New York, NY: Random House.

Matthay, T. (1913). *The art of touch*. London, UK: Longmans.

McPherson, G., & Davidson, J. (2006). Playing an instrument. In G. McPherson (Ed.), *The child as musician* (pp. 331–351). Oxford, UK: Oxford University Press.

Pink, D. (2009). *Drive: The secret truth about what motivates us*. New York, NY: Riverhead Books.

Rabin, R. (1996). *At the beginning: Teaching piano to the very young child*. New York, NY: Schirmer Books.

Rudney, G. L. (2005). *Every teacher's guide to working with parents*. Thousand Oaks, CA: Corwin Press.

Sloboda, J. (1993). Musical ability. In *The origins and development of high ability*. West Sussex, UK: Wiley.

Spock, B. (1946). *The common sense book of baby and child care*. New York, NY: Duell, Sloan, and Pearce.

Stitt, N., & Brooks, N. (2014). Reconceptualizing parent involvement: Parent as accomplice or parent as partner? *Schools: Studies in Education, 11*(1), 75–101.

Thompson, M. B. (2014). "Don't' rush, but don't rest": Reflections on Dr. Suzuki's affirmative guidance. *American Suzuki Journal, 43*(1), 46–48.

Thompson, M. B. (2015). Peers, tension, and more: Reflections on working with Suzuki parents. *American Suzuki Journal, 43*(2), 64–66.

Thompson, M. B. (2016a). Pictures of parents. *American Suzuki Journal, 44*(2), 82–85.

Thompson, M. B. (2016b). Understanding and nurturing parents. *American Music Teacher*. February/March, 25–29.

Tutwiler, S. J. (2005). *Teachers as collaborative partners*. Mahwah, NJ: Lawrence Erlbaum Associates.

Vincent, C. (1996). *Parents and teachers: Power and participation*. London, UK: Falmer Press.

Wallis, W. (1932). *The sociology of teaching*. New York, NY: Russell & Russell.

Chapter 8
Coda

Abstract This final chapter invites music teachers to fuel the flourishing of independent and authentic student musicians. This means being attentive to three important dynamics: helping students to recognize and value their achievements, building on students' reflective feedback, and purposefully uncovering and empowering what genuinely motivates students to learn. Additionally, teachers' capacity for fuelling authentic student musicians may be influenced by deeply understanding their own formative pedagogic experiences, by critically examining their ongoing role in teaching, and by teachers exercising the spectrum of their own potential and imagination. Finally, *Fundamentals of Piano Pedagogy* calls teachers to consider the legacy of music lessons and what they want their students and themselves to take away from the weeks, months, and years of musical explorations still to come.

Nathan's Notebook (January 11, 2013 to March 22, 2017)—Just over four years of weekly entries have passed since I wrote in Nathan's notebook at the end of his first lesson. As I turn to the notebook's last page, I realize it's the perfect time to take Nathan on a brief tour and revisit some of the moments captured in the 200+ pages of my own writing. Of course, we find the names of pieces, the predictable entries related to bar 7 of a certain composition, challenges of the week, and keeping the beat for lots more pieces. Other entries call for imagination, artistry, beauty, thinking ahead, swinging the rhythm, flow, energy, spirit helpers, and tricks of the day. Revisiting the words helps us with pulling out memories of distant and recent lessons. We marvel that time has gone by so quickly and that Nathan has accomplished so much musically and personally. I write today's date on the final page and underneath in bold letters—4 YEARS BRAVO!

A central idea of *Fundamentals of Piano Pedagogy* has been how teaching encompasses multiple layers of teacher involvement. Teaching beginner piano students involves an attentiveness to musical concerns like our relation with music,

© The Author(s) 2018
M.B. Thompson, *Fundamentals of Piano Pedagogy*,
SpringerBriefs in Education, DOI 10.1007/978-3-319-65533-8_8

learning to play by ear and by reading, caring for music, the importance of tone and technique, and helping students develop fluency through their accumulated repertoire. Teaching beginner piano students also draws from personal undercurrents like independence and authenticity, the moral and ethical dignity associated with democratic relationships, and meaningful conversations with parents. Furthermore, another layer of teaching beginners acknowledges both sides of a coin in terms of growth and rest, teaching *what is* and *what might be*, as well as advocating and agitating student development. In this view, what teachers do from the beginning is a reflection of their life knowledge and musical expertise. Their teaching is intimately connected to the closely held beliefs and personal values that permeate teachers' thoughts and actions in everyday life.

My purpose in bringing together these various layers of teaching has been to provide a pedagogical opening for piano, vocal, and instrumental teachers to consider their own teaching. This process begins with teachers finding their own place within the text, identifying how certain *fundamentals* synchronize with their own autobiography of personal and professional experiences. It's all about those "aha" moments when teachers intentionally and unintentionally respond to what they're reading. On certain occasions, they may take ownership of ideas, even going so far as to profess, "That's what I do", "That makes sense", or "I've always wanted to include that". Such statements confirm feelings of reassurance and competency. On other occasions, teachers may also proclaim, "Why didn't I think of that before?" or "How can I possibly incorporate that idea?" They acknowledge the challenges of integrating minimally familiar and previously unknown ideas.

Fundamentals of Piano Pedagogy isn't merely a collection of ideas supported by research and my own lengthy pedagogic career. Rather, I've written this book to serve both as a teaching resource and as a catalyst for teachers engaged in teaching from the beginning. Much like the way looking through Nathan's Notebook offered him glimpses of himself as a pianist, the topics contained herein may have offered teachers similar glimpses into the many layers of their own teaching. And just as Nathan's Notebook relied on Nathan and me to make sense of what was written, this book also relies on teachers to make meaning by interpreting the text and interrogating their own pedagogical approach. Undoubtedly, this is a complex, personal, and demanding undertaking that continues beyond reading this book from cover to cover; much like the way Nathan's musical journey has still more to experience in future explorations, performances, and conversations. This pedagogic undertaking is immensely worthwhile, in particular because it prepares teachers to stimulate something quite remarkable—namely, the *flourishing* of students.

8.1   Flourishing

What seems clear in teaching beginner piano students is that teachers may fuel the *flourishing* of students. For me, the word flourishing stands out because of its momentum and positive direction. The energy in flourishing is indicative of thriving, possibly involving adventure and risk, without losing sight of our own contemplative thought processes. Flourishing conjures up images of living the good life, of autonomy, mastery, and personal growth that's always evolving and changing. Flourishing individuals are highly motivated. They actively pursue new goals, and possess broad skills and resources. Personal health is also implicated in flourishing, including the wellbeing of heart and mind, our emotions, body and soul, our intellectual capacity, even our imagination and character.

Piano teachers have ample opportunity for the cultivation of students' flourishing because they connect with students on a weekly basis for periods that may last several years. So—How can piano teachers promote flourishing of their beginner students? What's involved? I suggest three important dynamics that demand teachers' attention: personal achievement, self-awareness, and individual potential. These three dynamics are by no means the sum total of what student flourishing may entail, but their interweaving provides an outline for meaningful consideration.

A first condition—the flourishing of students' personal achievement/experience—begins with teachers helping students to recognize and value their own successes. Teachers provide ongoing guidance for students in internalizing their accomplishments through refinement of their accumulated repertoire. They mentor rather than monitor their students. Because teachers incorporate the overlapping processes of leading, handing over, and expanding, students gradually acquire and apply increasingly sophisticated skills to their learning and performing.

Regarding a second domain—the flourishing of students' self-awareness/reflection—teachers prompt students' exploration of musicianship from a multiple ownership perspective. They promote students' capacity for reflection by welcoming and building on students' feedback. They use descriptive rather than judgmental language to communicate. Teachers invite students to meaningfully examine the contrasts and similarities between various models, including students' own interpretations and their teachers' preferred approach to performance.

A third condition—the flourishing of students' individual potential/imagination—involves teachers' commitment to uncovering and empowering what genuinely motivates students to learn. Because teachers accept their own musical journey is not their students' musical journey, they're comfortable with teaching what students want to know (advocacy) without relinquishing what students would benefit from learning (agitation). They're curious to see where students' character, creativity, emotions, and imagination will take them.

Teachers who fuel student flourishing may also unconsciously fuel their own flourishing as teachers. Both student growth and teacher flourishing may be profoundly influenced by teachers having a deep understanding of their own achievements and experiences, by teachers participating in the critical awareness and reflection of their role in teaching, and by teachers exercising a spectrum of potential and imagination.

Regarding the first condition—because teachers have deep understandings, they're able to use their achievements/experiences as fertile resources to share with students, rather than inflexible or unquestionable standards students must adopt. Flourishing teachers intuitively transform the fundamentals of piano pedagogy into meaningful explorations for their students, often bringing in stories, images, and metaphors that match students' personalities and life experiences. They know that their achievements/experiences make for good starting points, not end points.

A second domain—because teachers critically reflect on their teaching role, they're able to detect what's working and what's not working in their teaching. This aspect has two distinct variations. On a detailed level, teachers recognize how the specific characteristics of an activity may engage or fail to engage students. On a broader level, teachers notice how patterns of student growth or lack of growth resulting from their teaching may emerge over several weeks or months. Flourishing teachers think about how they teach before, during, and after their students' lessons. As a result of critical awareness and reflection into the details and patterns of piano pedagogy, they don't hesitate to modify their approach with numerous possibilities.

Regarding a third condition—teachers' potential and imagination—flourishing teachers are both resourceful and adaptive. They view their potential for growth as evolving and changing. Because they're secure in their own autonomy and possess a high degree of motivation, they readily seek out information and resources to extend their own skills and understanding of piano pedagogy. They elevate their teaching by welcoming the imaginative input of colleagues, friends, family, and above all their students. When flourishing teachers encounter uncertainties and unknowns in teaching, they have the courage and curiosity to try out completely opposite and previously unexplored directions.

8.2 Final Thoughts

On the evening before I started writing these final pages, one of my closest friends inquired, "So, if you had to summarize the entire book in one statement, what would that statement be?" This is the phrase I came up with:

Fundamentals of Piano Pedagogy invites studio music teachers into a multilayered ear-before-eye pedagogic approach that fuels the flourishing of independent and authentic student musicians right from the very beginning.

As might be expected, teachers in a *Fundamentals* model bring vast amounts of musical and instructional knowledge to their teaching. However, effective teaching is more than having students diligently follow teachers' instructions in order to reproduce what teachers know. It's about teaching in which both teachers' and students' voices are heard not through patronizing superficial exchanges, but by teachers being curious about and genuinely valuing what students literally and musically have to say.

Studio music teaching seems to be approaching an important crossroads—one where teachers will need to decide whether to continue along the path they've always known or turn onto a route that seems potentially inviting yet remains somewhat unknown. For individuals with traditional backgrounds, the problem with changing routes is that much of their success may be attributed to students diligently following teachers' instructions, even though an equally impressive number of students may have quit music lessons to escape following teachers' instructions. Admittedly, when I hear an adult say, "I took piano lessons as a child and absolutely hated it," I nod my head, knowing exactly what they're talking about. Yet, I can't help imagining a future alternative where an adult might say, "I took piano lessons as a child and absolutely loved it. It's amazing how five minutes at the piano after work can improve my day." Somehow, it doesn't seem unreasonable to think that a *Fundamentals* teaching approach could help studio music teachers achieve such an outcome.

At a most basic level, *Fundamentals of Piano Pedagogy* is about teachers living and teaching with awareness, gratitude, and hope. It isn't about the search for perfectionism or the eradication of our self-perceived flaws. The themes presented in this book are reliable, they work in actual music studios, and incorporating them will bring teachers more in tune with what it means to flourish as studio music teachers. Most likely, it all starts with teachers letting go of what they see getting in the way and continues by teachers taking the time and making the effort for the fruits of their exploration to take shape.

In the end, the eight chapters contained in *Fundamentals of Piano Pedagogy* may present teachers with any number of routes for exploration. To indicate that exploring such routes might be easy seems boldly inaccurate. On the other hand, to imply the need for hard work seems overblown. My impression is that making the most from this book requires teachers' willingness to tolerate uncertainty and unpredictability, to maintain a healthy optimism and realistic expectations, and to hold onto challenging perspectives until they trigger new knowledge. Finally, these highly personal processes of ongoing learning also call teachers to think critically about the legacy of music lessons and what they may wish to accomplish in the future—to think about what they want their students and themselves to take away from the weeks, months, and years of music lessons still to come.

Index

A
Acceptable tension, 68, 69
Accumulated repertoire, 4, 61, 63, 65–67, 91, 93
Ahrens, Cora, 79
Allsup, Randall, 7, 36, 38
Arrau, Claudio, 56
Atkinson, G.D., 79
Authenticity *See* Personal authenticity

B
Background stage *See* Learning
Baskwill, Jane, 86
Bastien, James, 57, 79
Beliefs
    parent, 5
    teacher, 3, 38, 92
Breathing, 12, 21, 28, 40, 55, 56, 59
Breithaupt, Rudolf, 48
Byo, James, 27

C
Campbell, Patricia, 26
Camp, Max, 58, 64
Care theory, 70
Carey, Benedict, 10
Caring for music, 63, 70, 71, 91
Charaniya, Nadira, 68
Circles
    arm, 3, 47, 53, 54, 58
Claire, Leslie, 40
Clementi, Muzio, 37, 48
Coloroso, Barbara, 8, 76
Competency, 13, 64, 66, 71, 92
Compulsory public schooling, 37
Conservatory, 37, 38, 79, 87
Core, 5, 12, 48, 55, 56, 58, 76
Cortot, Alfred, 48

Csikszentmihalyi, Mihalyi, 6
Cumming, Naomi, 12
Curiosity *See* Interest
Czerny, Carl, 37, 48, 58

D
Davidson, Jane, 68, 85
Davis, Brent, 20, 25, 37, 62
De Lorenzo, Lisa, 36, 38
Dewey, John, 39, 68
Duke, Robert, 27, 66

E
Ear-before-eye, 23, 24, 94
Egbert, Marion, 79
Expertise, 1, 2, 4, 13–15, 41, 45, 67, 71, 77, 78, 81, 83, 91

F
Fingers
    grab and release, 49, 51
    walking, 3, 47, 51–54, 58
Flourishing, 14, 20, 71, 92–94
Flow, 6, 56, 57, 91
Foundation stage *See* Learning
Fraser, Alan, 52

G
Gabrielsson, Alf, 23, 31, 36
Gembris, Heiner, 68
Gieseking, Walter, 48
Gordon, Edwin, 24, 25
Grab and release *See* Fingers
Growth and rest, 33, 91

H
Hanon, Charles-Louis, 37

© The Author(s) 2018
M.B. Thompson, *Fundamentals of Piano Pedagogy*,
SpringerBriefs in Education, DOI 10.1007/978-3-319-65533-8

43689177R00062

Made in the USA
San Bernardino, CA
16 July 2019